Savage Paradise

Hugo van Lawick

Savage Paradise

The predators of Serengeti

William Morrow and Company, Inc.
New York
1977

By the same author

INNOCENT KILLERS
(with Jane Goodall)

SOLO:
The Story of an African Wild Dog

Copyright © 1977 by Hugo van Lawick

All rights reserved. No part of this book may be
reproduced or utilized in any form or by any
means, electronic or mechanical, including
photocopying, recording or by any information
storage and retrieval system, without permission
in writing from the Publisher. Inquiries should be
addressed to William Morrow and Company, Inc.,
105 Madison Avenue, New York, N.Y. 10016.

Printed in Great Britain by Westerham Press Ltd
Bound by R. J. Acford, Chichester, Sussex

Designed by Linda Sullivan

1 2 3 4 5 6 7 8 9 10

Library of Congress Catalog Card Number
77–78060

ISBN 0–688–03235–4

To my son, Hugo

I should like to express my sincere thanks to the many people who have made it possible for me to live and work amongst the animals in Tanzania. Many government officials, including those of the Tanzanian National Parks and of the Ngorongoro Crater Authority, have, at all times, encouraged me in my attempts to portray the splendour of their country.

My thanks are also due to George Dove and Chimanbhai Patel, the respective owners of the Ndutu Lodge, who, by taking care of my supplies, made it possible for me to establish my camp at Lake Ndutu. In addition their staff never failed to help me when I needed it.

My gratitude is also due to a great number of friends who helped me in a variety of ways with my work. I should specifically like to mention Patricia Moehlman, James Malcolm, Diana Saltoon, Gerald Rilling, Aadje Geertsema, and George and Lory Frame.

CONTENTS

Introduction

I was fifteen when I shot my first film material on wild animals. I was using 8mm film, but I didn't know that and I had no idea what all those strange numbers on the lens meant. Yet I was on my first wildlife film assignment and I crept stealthily on my belly through the blueberry plants towards a wild Mouflon sheep in a National Park in Holland. Hidden in the bushes behind me, my ten friends wondered whether I would reach a predetermined spot; for the lens had been preset for distance and I had no idea how to refocus it. In short, I knew nothing about photography and had only been chosen because I was an expert at creeping on my belly towards animals.

After this experience I established a wildlife filming team with three of my friends. This kept us busy for a few summer holidays, during which time I learnt some of the basic facts about photography. I had always wanted to work with animals. Now I knew how.

On leaving school and completing my national service in the army, I set about my future. I enquired about film schools, but there were not many in those days and such as did exist were prohibitively expensive. So I had to give up that idea. Instead I applied for a job in Dollywood, a film company in Amsterdam where, as the name implies, films were made using puppets. The company was run by Joop Geesink, a great, jovial man who exuded enthusiasm from every pore, and he took me on as an assistant cameraman for one of his teams.

My home in Amersfoort was too far from my new work for me to travel there every day and so I had to find a place to live in Amsterdam. I was lucky, for I met an old school-friend who invited me to share his artist's studio. It was in a backstreet, and after chaining our bicycles to a lamp-post we had to climb four flights of dark, creaky stairs which wound their way through the narrow building to our attic. It was spacious but grimy and unfinished paintings cluttered the corners. Judging by the cobwebs which covered them, they must have been antiques. The rent for our home came to £3 per month which, even in those days, was cheap. On the second floor of the building lived an unmarried young lady of questionable profession with her five children. I made sure my mother never visited me, for I doubted whether she would have appreciated the environment.

As an assistant cameraman I was paid to clean the camera, put it on the tripod and so on. I was not, of course, allowed to film with it, but by watching the cameramen at work and discussing film-making with the experts in the studio, I learnt much during that first year. To my dismay I discovered it might take over five years for me to become a cameraman. I was in a hurry to start filming animals and, in the hope of hastening my education, not only studied every book on photography that I could lay my hands on, but also saved up to buy a simple 16mm camera. Later I realized this was a mistake. It would have been cheaper to buy a still camera or 8mm camera, and I would then have been able to afford more film material and thus get more experience.

At this time the most popular wildlife series on television was Armand and Michaela Denis's *On Safari*. One day my mother phoned. She had read in the newspaper that the Denises were visiting Amsterdam and had arranged for me to meet them. I did not fool myself that they would offer me a job. My experience was insufficient. My feelings were accentuated when Armand asked how many thousands of feet of film I had shot. I was amazed. I had never thought in thousands of feet – I couldn't afford to. Armand suggested I should try to find a job in Africa – any job – and then get some filming experience in my free time. He had some business to attend to that evening, but Michaela accepted my mother's invitation to supper and asked to see some of my film material. Luckily she was impressed with the little I had got and so a year later I joined the Denises in Africa.

During the next two years I completed a number of assignments for the Denises' *On Safari* series, the most dangerous of which involved the filming of wild-animal trappers catching rhinos. To do this I was perched precariously on the back of a truck which was driven at full speed cross-country in pursuit of a rhino. The driver ignored all but the largest objects in his path, whilst in the back of the truck next to me a tough-looking character held a long bamboo pole with a rope noose dangling from the end. The other end of the rope was tied to the truck. There were more, equally tough characters with us in the back, holding on for dear life as we raced cross-country and occasionally ducking as thornbush branches whipped low over the truck. One of them had lost an eye thanks to an inch-long thorn and, during one of the chases I was on, another man got a thorn right through his wrist. Finally, after various unsuccessful attempts, the man with the pole managed to slip the noose over a rhino's neck. At this the driver slowed down and stopped. The rope went taut and the rhino was brought to a standstill. The peace was momentary, the rhino charged and the truck shuddered when it was hit by the large beast. Moments later the side of the car was being lifted from the ground. There was pandemonium as people scrambled around me and it took all my concentration to keep filming what was going on. Suddenly the truck fell to the ground and some of the men rushed forward and shortened the rope. Now the rhino was stuck alongside. More ropes were put around it and one man jumped out and tied its hind-legs. The rhino was a captive and I felt sorry for it.

Photographing under such conditions may be an art, but the results are rarely artistic. It is what I call journalistic photography – recording events as fast as possible under extremely difficult circumstances. This is often necessary during wildlife photography – even when filming animals which are not being put upon like the unfortunate rhino. One may only have a split second of warning that an animal is about to do something exciting and, unless one can react quickly, it will be too late.

When I left the Denises and started life as a freelance cameraman, I owned a good film camera, six lenses and enough money to survive for a month. It didn't give me much leeway but I soon found I was in the right place at the right time. Hearing I was looking for work, Dr Louis Leakey invited me to stay at his house outside Nairobi. At the time his wife Mary was searching for fossils at the Olduvai Gorge. Prehistory had been a hobby of mine for many years and I was delighted to have the opportunity to talk to Dr Leakey about his work. He had tremendous enthusiasm and took an almost boyish delight in instilling it into younger people. He held the belief that females were generally better observers than males, but ultimately decided that I was an exception to his rule.

I felt at home in the Leakeys' house. There were animals all over the place: antelopes which had been rescued as orphans, a cat with two different-coloured eyes (one green, one blue), dogs, fishes which Louis bred, a tortoise and, at the bottom of the garden in a pit, some highly poisonous snakes which had been collected by his eldest son, Jonathan. A gigantic python lived next to the kitchen and a tree hyrax, a small nocturnal creature which looks a bit like a rabbit with short ears, lived in the roof above my bedroom. Regularly throughout the night it made a sound like a pig being strangled, a feature of African life which took a bit of getting used to.

I had only been at the house for two days when the phone rang – a call from the USA for Dr Leakey. It was the President of the National Geographic Society. A lecture film was needed on Dr Leakey's work. Did he know of a cameraman available immediately? A few days later, Louis and I were on our way to the Olduvai Gorge and I shot my first material for the National Geographic.

Life as a freelance photographer had started well, but would the powers that be at the Geographic like my material and give me further work? Part of the answer was soon provided, for I got a telegram asking whether I would consider flying to Washington to discuss the possibility of further assignments – air fare and expenses would be paid.

My visit to Washington got off to a bad start because the first question put to me was whether I could take still photographs of the quality needed for the

Society's famous magazine. Since my experience had mainly been in filming, I wasn't sure. I was handed a camera and told to prove myself by photographing people in Washington. I was horrified. I was a wildlife photographer and, being shy by nature, hesitated to point my camera at people unknown to me. My experiences that day did nothing to help. I will not go into them, except to mention that I got some nasty looks from a young man when I photographed his pretty young lady looking at the monkeys in the Washington Zoo. Feeling dejected and even less sure of myself amongst people, I returned to the Society's headquarters.

Next day they sent an experienced photographer with me. We went to a small shipyard where sailing boats were being built. My guide spoke to the manager of the yard who, to my delight, informed the men working on the boats that I would be photographing them. This time there could be no misunderstandings and I happily started taking pictures.

'Hey, mister, where do you come from?' asked one of the men.

'East Africa,' I replied, taking another picture.

'Been close to wild animals?'

'Sure,' I replied. Some of the other men had paused and were listening. They were obviously interested and I felt pleased. I was getting a good rapport with them.

'How close have you been to a rhino?'

Thinking of the occasion I had filmed the capture of a rhino, I said, 'Touching distance.'

It was fatal. There were snorts of disbelief and from then on the men ignored me.

I longed to be back in the African bush. This wish was soon granted, for the National Geographic gave me various film and still photography assignments. Having obtained a loan, I bought a Land-Rover when I got back to Africa and quickly got to work.

Almost immediately I learnt an important lesson. I needed photographs of Jonathan Leakey's work in his snake farm in the north of Kenya. I photographed him catching a cobra; then took pictures of him milking an enormous Gaboon viper, curving its large fangs over the edge of a dish and extracting the poison, which would be used in the production of snake-bite serum.

As he was doing this, one of his assistants rushed up with the news that he had seen a large python disappearing down a burrow in the ground. When we got to the spot some time later, Jonathan strapped a band around his head on to which a lamp was attached. He looked remarkably like a miner. Taking a large sack, he disappeared down the den, only to reappear a minute later, crawling backwards and covered in sand. I could see the bag was empty. Turning round, he said: 'It's down there. The burrow's not very deep but it makes a ninety-degree turn six feet down, and he's just around the corner – maybe three feet further.'

Jonathan gave his two Kenyan assistants some instructions in Swahili, which I didn't understand, and prepared to disappear again.

'Wait,' I said suddenly. 'Mind if I crawl down there first and get some pictures?'

'Go ahead,' he replied.

I put a small flash on my camera and pre-set the diaphragm and the distance on the lens at two feet. Jonathan handed me his miner's lamp which I strapped on to my head before I disappeared into the bowels of the earth. I didn't feel I needed to look the snake in the eyes, so I didn't go very far. Seeing the ninety-degree turn which Jonathan had mentioned, I stopped, held the camera around the corner and pressed the button. There was a blinding flash and I could hear the snake puffing itself up and hissing loudly. Fumbling in the enclosed space, I changed the flash bulb, adjusted the focus and diaphragm to three feet and took another picture. I repeated this a number of times and then crawled out. Handing Jonathan his miner's lamp, I thanked him. He looked at me and said softly but with emphasis: 'I wouldn't have done that.' Seeing me look puzzled, he added: 'I always hold the sack in front of me. Although they're not poisonous, they have very sharp teeth. Sorry, I thought you realized.'

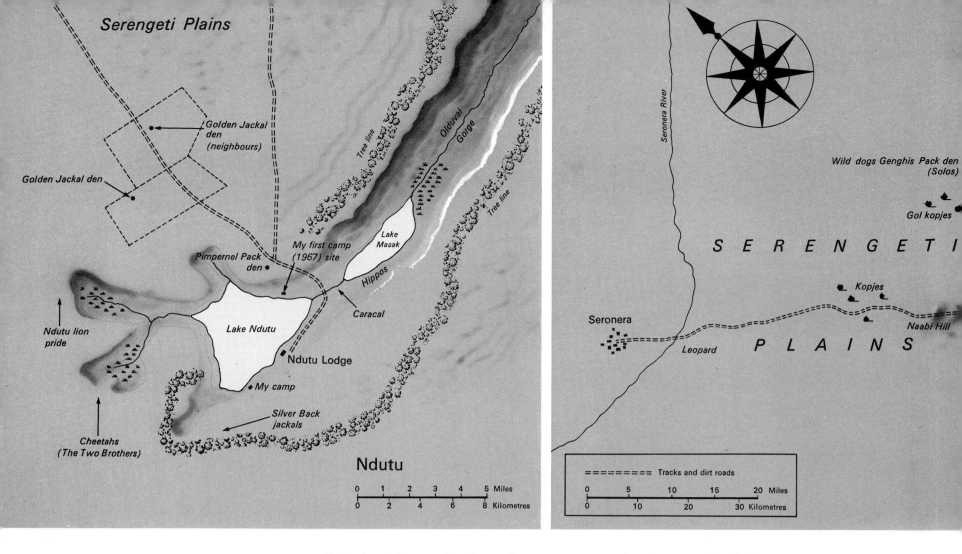

So I should have, but in my keenness to get the pictures, I hadn't thought. It was a good lesson for the future. Of course, when photographing wildlife, one regularly takes risks. It's part of the job. But they should always be calculated ones, not thoughtless actions. If I had been sensible I would still have gone down that den, but I would first have wrapped a cloth around my hands. Since then I have become somewhat of a stickler for safety precautions, often to the annoyance of students I have worked with. However, it is stupid to die or be mutilated unnecessarily and when one has lived in the wild for a while, it is easy to be lulled into a false sense of security and to forget what dangers are all around.

One must always be on the alert. I have had my share of close escapes: for instance, lions tried to creep up on me as I was working; a rhino charged through my camp; a leopard tore my tent whilst I was asleep; I woke to find a large, poisonous snake lying beside me; I sank to my middle in a quicksand; I was bitten by a chimpanzee in my neck, a millimetre from my jugular vein, and so on. Yet one of the closest escapes I had was when an elephant charged me while I was on a visit to America. It was an African elephant that had attacked its keeper, and I was trying to come to the rescue. We survived, but I remember being convinced that my last moment had come and thinking how ridiculous it was to be killed by an elephant in the United States.

The most dangerous and exciting job I have done regularly is to follow animals such as wild dogs or hyenas on moonlit nights, racing along with them cross-country while they hunt, at speeds of between 30 and 45 m.p.h. One cannot use headlights because this would disturb the animals. Trying to anticipate the dangers of the terrain, such as the innumerable potholes, whilst at the same time keeping an eye on the animals, involves instant reactions and every nerve and sense being strained to its limits. I once took a student on such night work and a year later his father told me that his son had written about the adventure: 'An incredible experience. Hugo was driving in the dark, cross-country at 30 m.p.h. while the hyenas chased their prey. He was driving with one hand, for in the other he held his camera which he occasionally stuck out of the window to take a picture, the strobe-lights having been attached to the car. In addition to this, he somehow managed to light a cigarette!'

The five years I worked for the National Geographic Society as a film and still photographer provided me with invaluable and much-needed experience. I now wanted to be able to express myself more fully than I could as a cameraman, for both film-making and still photography involve team work to a greater or lesser extent. The cameraman is but a 'cog in the wheel' and normally has little or no say in how his material is used. It can hardly be otherwise, for he is unlikely to be an expert in the various fields needed to complete a film or, for that matter, a magazine article. Many cameramen, indeed, do not wish to be involved in anything beyond

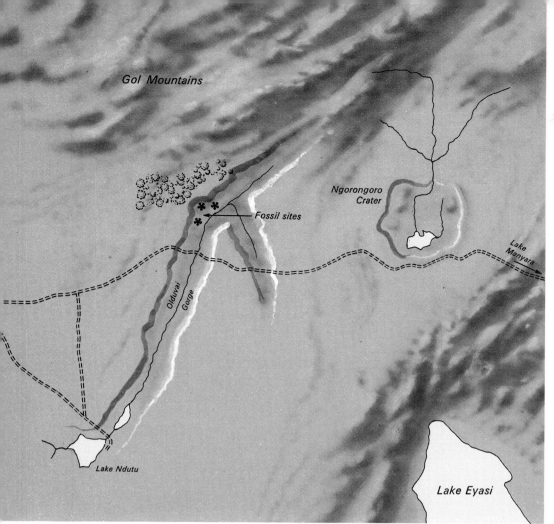

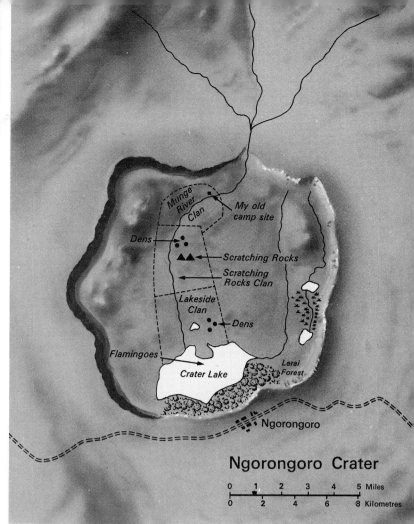

Gol Mountains

Fossil sites

Ngorongoro
Crater

Lake
Manyara

Olduvai
Gorge

Lake Ndutu

Lake Eyasi

Munge
River
Clan

My old
camp site

Dens

Scratching Rocks

Scratching
Rocks Clan

Lakeside
Clan

Dens

Flamingoes

Lerai
Forest

Crater Lake

Ngorongoro

Ngorongoro Crater

0 1 2 3 4 5 Miles
0 2 4 6 8 Kilometres

the camera work, but I found the limitation frustrating. It was obvious that I would have to try to do something independently. However, I faced the problem that perplexes almost every would-be film maker. I didn't have sufficient funds to finance a film myself, nor could I hope that anyone else would put up the money, for of course I had no proof that I could do more than just camera work.

At this stage, the late Sir William Collins encouraged me to write a book in partnership with my former wife, Jane Goodall. The book, on hyenas, jackals and wild dogs, was to contain many photographs and to be based on original observation. Whilst Jane concentrated on hyenas, I studied jackals and wild dogs. I will not here go into details of the two-year research which resulted in the book, *Innocent Killers*. Suffice it to say that it led to my making a film on wild dogs which won six awards and established me as an independent film maker. It also resulted in another book, *Solo: The Story of an African Wild Dog*, and a contract to make three more one-hour films for television in the USA. Film making is my principal occupation yet I shall never give up still photography, for I believe that it can produce results quite as informative and as beautiful as any moving picture.

By now I have lived in Africa for sixteen years. Home to me is not a house, it is my camp on the Serengeti overlooking Lake Ndutu. It is a spacious camp, consisting of a dining tent, an office tent, a kitchen, my bedroom tent and various tents for guests who have named my camp 'Hugo's Hilton'. Certainly it has many comforts, such as a fridge, easy chairs, comfortable beds and superb food prepared by my excellent cook, who with an assistant takes care of the camp when I am away. With a menu like smoked sailfish as a starter, followed by a soup, then duck (*à l'orange*) with a bottle of Châteauneuf-du-Pape, it is no wonder my camp is popular with some of the local inhabitants, in particular the hyenas and jackals. At first I used a tent for a kitchen, but after a number of my meals had been stolen, I had a hyena-proof kitchen built. This camp is, of course, too large to move around easily. It is my base, and when I need to work elsewhere, as I often do, I take one or two small tents and rough it, as used to be my normal way of living.

When I first arrived at Ndutu in 1967 in order to study wild dogs, I had not planned to stay longer than six months. However, I soon became so fascinated by the behaviour of the wild dogs that I continued work on them for a number of years. And so the area became my home. At the same time, I got to know many of the other animals around Ndutu, such as a pride of lions that lives there, two cheetahs which regularly roam the area, various families of Golden Jackals and so on. The more I see of them the more I want to know each individual better. In addition, the surroundings of Ndutu are beautiful and varied, giving me plenty of scope for my photography. The lake is sometimes pink with flamingoes and peaceful, at other times filled with drama, as when the wildebeest migration crosses it and individuals drown or calves lose their mothers. Around the lake the acacia trees, their gnarled branches silhouetted against the sky, provide shade under their flat tops for many creatures, such as herds of impala, a few rhinos, and many pairs of diminutive dikdiks, antelopes scarcely larger than a hare.

In some places, too, there is almost impenetrable bush country. This is the home of the rarely seen Striped Hyenas. Beyond this the vast plains stretch away to the horizon, sometimes bleak and hostile, sometimes a sea of green grass covered with flowers and millions of animals. Snaking away from Lake Ndutu is the Olduvai Gorge, and where the gorge ends the country rises towards the Ngorongoro Crater, a three- to four-hour drive from my camp. There are many other areas of interest within easy driving reach of the camp. For instance, to the North-East lie the Gol Mountains and to the North-West Seronera, the centre of the Serengeti, where I watch leopards.

My day-to-day work involves getting up before sunrise, the time depending on which animal I hope to find and how far it lives from my camp. The lions and cheetahs are usually within eight miles and sometimes on my doorstep, so I start my search when the sun rises. On the other hand, if I am photographing a den of dogs twenty miles away I have to set off at the first light of dawn.

The most interesting examples of animal behaviour, to some extent depending on the species, usually occur in the early morning or late afternoon. However, I stay out all day and in fact have made some of the most surprising discoveries at about midday: for instance, that Egyptian Vultures throw stones at ostrich eggs and that leopards often hunt at that time, when the gazelles are somewhat drowsy. In general the predators tend to sleep most of the day and it can become boring waiting for them to wake up and do something, but such intervals give me the opportunity to watch some of the other creatures, such as birds. It was at such a time, to mention only one case, that I noticed that a small bird, the wheatear, which often lives near the dens of jackals and wild dogs, seems to imitate some of the sounds of these two species.

I have passed on this information to an ornithological expedition from Cambridge University, which will study the behaviour in more detail, for first and foremost I am a photographer, not a scientist. However, by living on the Serengeti and having spent tens of thousands of hours observing wild animals, I could not help but become an expert on some of the creatures I have watched. To introduce my photographs, therefore, I have written six brief chapters, first on the large cat-like predators, lions, leopards and cheetahs (which are not true cats), and then on the dog-like ones, the Spotted Hyenas (which strangely may be more closely related to cats), jackals and wild dogs. These essays are not intended as scientific monographs, but are rather a description of my own involvement with each species and of some of the remarkable things that happened while I was watching them.*

My photographs, I hope, will reflect the love I have for the Serengeti and the Ngorongoro Crater and inspire this in others; but in an honest way, for with its beauty there is also harshness, a savage struggle to survive in a paradise.

---

* Scientists who have studied carnivores on the Serengeti and in the Ngorongoro Crater are:
George Schaller, Brian Bertram, David & Jeannette Bygott: LIONS.
George Frame: CHEETAHS.
Hans Kruuk, Jane Goodall: HYENAS.
Patricia Moehlman: JACKALS.
James Malcolm, Lory Frame: WILD DOGS.

Lions

The animal which most visitors to East Africa want to see above all others is the lion. As a result, lions in areas frequented by tourists have become so used to cars that they are easy to approach and follow when on the move. In other areas, though, they may be quite timid and become disturbed when approached by a vehicle.

When watching a pride of lions, one often has a strange feeling that they are tame and that it would be quite safe to get out of the car. Some people have done this, and some of them did not survive, for lions can move deceptively fast and their reactions are unpredictable to those who have not studied them.

I have observed lions, on and off, throughout my sixteen years in Africa, but it was not until I made a film about a pride at Ndutu, that I really watched them intensively over a period of six months.

However, I had already got to know some of the lions in the area quite well, which was not surprising since I live in their territory. In fact it is common for lions to visit my camp, especially at night. Usually they just wander through but sometimes they may hunt there. This year one of the lionesses caught a wildebeeste a few yards in front of my bedroom tent. This is to be expected – the lions in this area are protected and so have nothing to fear from man. On the other hand humans are not protected, and I must admit that I do not always feel completely at ease when walking in the dark with only the narrow beam of a torch to light the way from my dining to my bedroom tent, a distance of some thirty yards. However, so far the lions at Ndutu have never bothered me.

A pride consists of one or more adult males and a number of females with their offspring. The adult females seem to be closely related; sisters, fully grown female offspring and so on. The adult males, which from my observations can number one to six, are probably brothers but have come from another pride, for male offspring, once they are about two years old, are driven out of the pride of their birth. This behaviour obviously avoids inbreeding within a pride. Whilst female offspring normally remain in the pride, some are driven out or leave, possibly when a pride becomes too large.

Individuals that leave a pride become nomadic. When young males are driven out, they continue to associate closely with each other. This is advantageous to them, for once full-grown they may try to take over a pride from resident males and, obviously, the more brothers there are to back each other up, the more likely they are to succeed. Some males never manage to take over a pride, however, and so remain nomads throughout their life, as apparently do the nomadic females.

Within a pride each member can wander around on its own all over a hunting range, or if it prefers, can join up into a temporary group with any of the other members. However, some individuals associate more frequently with each other than with others; thus the adult males can often be found together and females with cubs will tend to form a nursery group. It is rare to see all the members of a pride together at the same time.

I remember one pride particularly well. The two male lions had a problem – four of the females in their pride had come into heat at the same time. At first glance it appeared that the dominant male had taken possession of three females while one female had been left to the subordinate male. However, the situation was not quite like that.

The subordinate male was more or less on top of his situation. I say more or less because his female was of a fickle nature – she continually tried to slip past him and join the dominant male. Thus the subordinate male was kept busy blocking her way.

The dominant male on the other hand was far from on top. He was keen to mate with the dominant female but, unfortunately for him, she was not interested. On most occasions that he attempted to mate her, she would lie on her side and go to sleep; or at least pretend to. However, sometimes she would let the male mount her, giving all the indications that she wanted to be mated, but the moment he was ready, she would shoot away from under him, leaving him poised in mid-air and looking somewhat ridiculous. This was frustrating to say the least. However, the dominant male still had two other females to choose from and they were both exceedingly keen to be mated. As is typical of friendly felines, they tried to entice the male by rubbing themselves against him, soothingly and smoothly. Then they lay in front of him in the mating position. No matter how much they tried, the male was only interested in the dominant female, which continued to reject him in spite of his untiring efforts. This in its turn frustrated the other two females, which became more and more importunate in their attempts to seduce the male. It did not help him to lie on his side and close his eyes; the two females continued to rub their lithe bodies along his back, over his head and down his tummy and even, at times, to push their rumps under his nose or lie half over him. In spite of his obvious annoyance at their persistence, the lion rarely lost his temper. Usually he growled softly or attempted to push the females away with one of his paws. However, this did little to deter them.

In the meantime the subordinate male occasionally mated his female and spent the rest of his time trying to stop her joining the others. At times his female would go to sleep or at least pretend to, but the moment he too relaxed, she would try to slip past him. It was obvious that the situation was making him nervous; all the more since he seemed to suspect that the dominant male might suddenly rush to the female's aid and steal her. I very much doubt whether the dominant male had any such intention, for he had enough problems to cope with already. On the other hand, he did frequently glare threateningly towards the subordinate male, but I suspect that he in turn was worried lest the other lion might sneak up and steal his favourite female. All in all, there was considerable confusion and tension.

It was not surprising that, by the time the two males had tried to cope with this situation for four days, they looked somewhat tired. Then the inevitable happened. The subordinate male closed his eyes for a bit too long and his female slipped past him and joined the others. Her mate did not give her up that easily. Having woken up, he rushed forward with a roar. The dominant male, seeing him approach the females, jumped to his feet and attacked. Rearing up on their hind legs the two males fought, clawing and biting at each other, their roars shattering the stillness of the plains. The fight was vicious but short, for the dominant male bit into the other's neck and, twisting sideways, threw him to the ground. When he let go, the subordinate male scrambled to his feet and fled, lying some distance away to lick his wounds and watch his female court the dominant male. From then on the dominant male was surrounded by three females, eager to be mated, but he rejected them all in favour of the dominant female who still seemed to need a lot of sleep.

I have never seen this sort of situation on any other occasion. Normally when a single lioness in a pride comes into heat, one of the males will mate with her whilst the other males watch from a distance, maybe waiting for an opportunity to take over. A male lion may court his female for as long as ten days, mating with her about one hundred times every twenty-four hours.

When a lioness is about to give birth, she likes to find a secluded spot such as the middle of some thick vegetation or a cave. Here she has her cubs. For the first four weeks of their life she keeps them hidden, but subsequently she may join the nursery group. Once in the group the mothers share the duty of caring for the cubs, to the extent that the youngsters can suckle from any female in milk. In fact I have often wondered whether, at this stage, cubs know which their real mother is. If so, it is not at all apparent.

Last year one of the lionesses I knew well gave birth to four cubs just below my camp. She had them well hidden in some thick bush and so I only caught a brief glimpse of them when they were two weeks old. I checked the area daily over the next fortnight but did not see them. However, I knew they were still there, for I could hear them greet their mother when she returned from a hunt. In the meantime I continued my photographic work on other animals in the area, planning to concentrate on the cubs when they emerged regularly.

Before they did so, I found some other members of the pride, three females lying at the edge of a marsh some five miles away. After a short while one of the lionesses left. As she looked thin, I guessed she was going to hunt. I'm not sure why I didn't follow her; in any case it proved a lucky decision. No sooner had she disappeared than one of the other lionesses got up and went into the reeds, emerging a minute later carrying a small cub by the scruff of its neck. Now the second lioness got up, following the first one as she carried the cub across the valley away from the marsh and then headed up a slope towards bush country. Having caught up, the second lioness walked parallel to the first, watching closely as the small cub, its face puckered, bounced slowly up and down by the scruff of its neck with every step the lioness took.

When they had gone half a mile, the first lioness headed for a thick bush where she deposited the cub. She gave it a few powerful licks over its face, which was barely larger than her tongue, and then headed back towards the marsh. I guessed she was planning to move all the cubs in the same way. The second female, however, had different ideas. She also gave the cub a few licks, then picked it up and carried it back to the marsh. The first lioness looked round and stopped but when the second lioness reached her, she let her pass and merely followed.

When the two lionesses reached the marsh, I could hear the sounds of more cubs hidden in the reeds. The second lioness did not take the lone cub to them but instead put it down in the open, near the edge of the marsh. For a moment the cub seemed lost but then, obviously encouraged by the sounds of its siblings, it turned and headed in their direction. With startling suddenness, a large paw landed on its back. A few seconds later it was once more being carried back to the thick bush half a mile away. As before, the second lioness followed and watched the small cub bouncing up and down in the first female's jaws. The whole procedure was then repeated; the cub was put down and, as soon as the first lioness had turned its back, the second carried it back to the marsh again.

Yet a third time the first lioness addressed itself to its task. By now, midday was approaching and both lionesses looked hot. When they reached the bush they lay down with the cub between them and spent the rest of the day there. However, just after sunset, the first lioness got up and headed for the marsh. The second one picked up the cub and followed her. As they reached the marsh the third lioness arrived. She had apparently been unsuccessful in her hunting, for she still looked thin. When she reached the edge of the marsh she called softly and one by one eleven small cubs emerged from the reeds. Soon these were joined by the lone cub looking none the worse for his frequent journeys. This time the first lioness did not try to take it back to the bush again.

When I revisited the marsh next morning, there was no sign of the lionesses, nor did I hear any sounds of the twelve cubs from the marsh. I guessed they had moved and so checked the bush to which the first lioness had repeatedly moved the lone cub the previous day. There was no sign of them there either. I spent the rest of the day searching the area extensively. When the sun set I reluctantly gave up and headed back towards my camp. There was still a little light left when I reached my tents and I decided to check up on the lone lioness with her four cubs. When I reached the spot, I found all four lionesses together, their sixteen cubs tumbling all over and around them. It was an amazing sight; all the more amazing since I realized that the three females from the marsh had, during the previous night, carried their cubs, one by one, for five miles to where they now were. From my tent that night I could occasionally hear the lionesses softly calling to their cubs.

When I returned to the four lionesses and their cubs the next morning, the cubs were suckling. All seemed peaceful except for an occasional squabble between two or three of the youngsters over the ownership of a nipple. Not far away a flock of guinea fowl searched for food amongst the grass, occasionally scratching up dust and pecking at whatever they had uncovered. In an acacia tree above the lions, two hooded vultures perched on a branch close together. They looked very much in love as they gently stroked each other's heads with preening beaks.

Suddenly one of the guinea fowl gave an alarm call and the flock ran off for a short distance. The lionesses looked up. Thirty yards away the vegetation slowly parted and a male lion with a beautiful thick mane appeared and walked towards them. When he reached a small thorn tree, he combed his mane through its lower branches and then continued towards the females and their cubs. Two of the lionesses got up and moved to meet him, making movements as if to rub heads with him, but instead they attacked, clawing at his face. With a roar the lion jumped backwards but the lionesses went after him, one thrusting a claw into his rump. The male roared again and then beat a hasty retreat. Rubbing heads with each other the two lionesses calmly walked back to the cubs. They would not tolerate a male too close to their youngsters.

Through the following weeks I noticed that, although the lionesses were aggressive towards two of the pride's males, they would tolerate the third one to a certain extent and allow him to rest fairly close to the cubs. The cubs were fascinated by this male and especially attracted by his mane, which they would sniff or pat. For his part the male showed no interest in the cubs and, in fact, seemed to be made ill-at-ease by their attentions. The cubs' well-being depended solely on the females.

When the cubs were eight weeks old the lionesses led them back to the marsh five miles from my camp where prey was more abundant. On arrival at the marsh, two of the lionesses were walking ahead. Suddenly I saw them run fast towards a giraffe which was grazing with head lowered among some bushes in a valley. I quickly grabbed my camera. Although I had photographed a young lion chasing a giraffe, I had never seen lions catch one. This time I felt sure that here was to be my chance. However, to my surprise, the lionesses stopped short and rushed up a tree. I soon found out why. A cloud of small, biting flies was upon them. The other lioness rushed up the tree as well, followed with some difficulty by the cubs. Evidently these flies belonged to the species which will not go above a certain height and I was thus the only prey left to them. When they had sucked enough blood they left, except for those which had fallen a victim to my frantic swatting.

It is often thought that only lions in certain areas, such as the Lake Manyara National Park, will climb and rest in trees. In fact I have seen lions do so in many areas, including the Ngorongoro Crater and the Serengeti. I have also heard scientists argue whether they climb trees to escape flies or for coolness. I believe they do so for both reasons. The lions at Ndutu and elsewhere frequently rested in trees even though there was no sign of biting flies. Blood-sucking flies can be more than just a nuisance. Not long ago there was a population explosion of such creatures in the Ngorongoro Crater and the lion population was decimated. However, this is rare. In many areas of East Africa, I have been less bothered by insects than in the forests of Europe, except for the normal non-biting flies which are to be found in great numbers on the Serengeti, especially when the zebras migrate past my camp.

Once the dry season started, it became clear that the four lionesses with their sixteen cubs had chosen well to live at the marsh, for many prey animals came to drink there. All the same the lions often went hungry and I regularly found them looking thin. One day as I watched them a warthog appeared on the scene, oblivious of the lions. The four lionesses immediately started to creep towards it and, as there was plenty of high vegetation to hide their approach, I felt they had a reasonably good chance. However, one of the cubs was too keen for a good meal. Rushing past the startled lionesses, it ran up to the bush behind which the warthog had disappeared. The cub was in the ideal position for making a kill, but I couldn't help laughing when the two met. The warthog was at least three times the bigger. On seeing the youngster it gave a snort and then calmly trotted away.

Whilst such an incident may seem amusing to the onlooker, it can result in death for the lions. During the following weeks of the dry season, hunting became increasingly difficult and, one by one, eight of the cubs died of starvation. Undoubtedly more would have died if it hadn't been for the flamingoes. Small flocks of these birds started to visit the marsh which contained a number of saline pools. Flamingo hunting nearly always took place in the early morning and looked almost dreamlike. In the early sun, the dry reeds varied in hue from a dark green to a deep red and all through the marsh thousands of dew-spattered spider's webs deflected the light in rainbow colours. The pink flamingoes would land in slow motion and gracefully feed, unaware of the tawny form creeping up on them until it suddenly rushed into the pool amidst a spray of water. There is not much meat on a flamingo but undoubtedly these hunts kept the pride going during the dry season.

When the short rains started at Ndutu, the four lionesses and their eight cubs left the marsh and wandered throughout their hunting area. Many gazelles had returned and so food was once more plentiful.

It was during the zebra migration that same year that I was watching a pride of lions which had made their home on a kopje. Kopjes are small islands of rocks which jut out of the surrounding countryside. Where they occur on the open plains, they look like islands or oases in a desert and, like oases, they provide a haven for vegetation, for animals and, in prehistoric times, for man. Probably the most common creature to be found on a kopje is the Agama Lizard, of which there are many varieties. Usually the female of the species is dull coloured, blending well with her surroundings. In contrast the males are often brilliantly coloured. I have frequently seen bright blue or green males with heads a ruby red. For lions, the kopjes provide a good vantage point from which to spot prey and often there is water in small pools hidden amongst the rocks.

The lions that I was watching at the kopje rested most of the time, hour in, hour out. It can get pretty boring watching lions sleep and at times I would have liked to follow their example. Even if my conscience had let me, however, I wouldn't have been able to; there were too many flies which had the nasty habit of walking over my face as soon as I remained still. Being sensitive to tickling I couldn't ignore them. They bothered the lions, too, for I could see their skin twitch and they continually flicked their ears to chase away the flies behind them. In addition, the lions usually slept with one paw draped protectively over their sensitive noses. Then I discovered that the lions had an ally. As they lay there Agama Lizards approached from all directions, at first hesitantly and shaking their heads nervously up and down, but finally jumping on to the resting cats and catching the flies off them. The lions ignored them, even when the lizards caught flies from behind their ears.

I was to see this type of behaviour again but the outcome was somewhat different. I was watching a large pride resting in the shade of a tree. In seeking the maximum of shade one of the lionesses had pushed right up against the trunk. In spite of the many flies crawling on her back, she was fast asleep. After a while I noticed an Agama Lizard creeping down the tree trunk, its body almost the same colour as the bark of the tree.

Suddenly it noticed the flies on the lioness's back and rushed forward. On reaching the lioness it remained motionless but, when a fly came within reach, it snapped it up with its powerful jaws. However, in doing so, the lizard nipped the sleeping lioness, which jumped straight into the air with a roar. At this the other twenty resting lions jumped to their feet and there was considerable confusion. I couldn't help laughing at the puzzled expression on the lioness's face as she looked around, trying to determine who had pinched her bottom.

Life is not always easy for lions. Their main problem, of course, is food. It is seldom realized that an over-abundance of prey can make hunting difficult for some of the predators, such as lions, since it is almost impossible to creep up on a large herd in which there are always some animals on the look-out. On the other hand where there are large herds, as during the wildebeeste migration, animals will die of disease or old age and give the lions an opportunity to scavenge. 'King of Beasts' or not, the lion is an opportunist and will always take advantage of an easy meal if it will save it the trouble and frequent frustration of a hunt.

Few hunts are successful, maybe one in five. I don't like seeing animals kill each other, but I must admit that I am fascinated watching a hunt when the stealth of the predator is pitched against the alertness of the prey. Some of the most spectacular hunts I have seen have ended in the prey making an almost miraculous escape.

I remember once watching a large herd of Thomson Gazelles approach a water-hole. They frequently stopped and looked around and sometimes, for no apparent reason, the gazelles in front would turn and walk back towards the plain. This is normal behaviour for Thomson Gazelles when they approach water where they know they are vulnerable. Ultimately five of the gazelles, either braver, thirstier, or more foolhardy than the others, reached the pool and started to drink. Soon the others followed their example. When the last one had disappeared down the slope towards the pool, a lioness emerged from a bush forty yards away and swiftly ran to the waterhole. As she got closer, she increased her speed, but she was still ten yards short of the slope when the first gazelles appeared, their thirst slaked and on the way back to the plain.

For a split second the gazelles froze, then they fled. Ignoring them, the lioness ran down the slope, meeting the other gazelles head-on. She hit out at a female gazelle which managed to jump sideways out of her reach. Then I saw a male gazelle run straight towards the lioness. When it reached her it hesitated a split second, then jumped straight over her. The lioness, however, had seen the gazelle and, rearing up on her hind legs, swiped at it with both paws in an embracing movement. The gazelle streaked through the embrace, with only millimetres to spare between the outstretched claws on either side of it.

Another time I filmed a lioness actually grabbing a zebra's rump between her front paws. Both animals were going at full speed at the time and, as the powerful zebra continued to forge ahead, the lioness half ran, half bounced behind it on her hindlegs. Twice the zebra kicked back at the lioness; the second time it hit her in the chest and the lioness was thrown into the air. By the time the lioness returned to earth, the zebra was way ahead. I expected that it would not stop running for a long time; however, it only went fifty yards before it checked, looked back and, at a jaunty trot, rejoined its herd. Looking through binoculars I could see no wounds on its rump, although undoubtedly the lioness's claws must have penetrated the skin.

Life can be hard for the healthy lion; how much worse it must be for the cripple. I remember well one young lioness which I used to know in the Ngorongoro Crater. She was a member of the Munge River pride. When she was a cub, hyenas got hold of her but she had been saved by her mother. By then, however, the hyenas had bitten off part of one hind-leg. When I knew her, the wound had healed, but it was painful to watch her hobbling along on three legs. All the same, she managed. When her mother gave birth to a new litter, she was about two years old. More than most other young females she seemed to take a keen interest in the cubs. I wondered how she would manage later with her own litter for, with her disability, I doubted if she would ever be able to hunt. I was soon proved wrong. Her first prey was a wildebeest calf and, when she had killed it, she collected her mother and the cubs so they could share it with her. But the young female never lived to bear her own cubs. When she made her next kill, a yearling wildebeest, hyenas surrounded the young lioness and tore her to bits.

Whilst the most common prey of lions on the Serengeti and in the Ngorongoro Crater are wildebeests, zebras and the various gazelles, they will tackle surprisingly large animals at times. I have already mentioned giraffe. In addition lions will hunt eland, hippos and buffalo. I have seen lions chase buffalo on a number of occasions but have only seen them kill a sick one. Usually, however, they will go out of their way to avoid buffalo and I once filmed a lone buffalo as it charged 22 lions, which hastily scattered in all directions.

Lions can move remarkably fast, as is illustrated by an incident observed by an assistant of mine some years ago. He was watching lions on the short grass plains, when some of them chanced on a large cobra. The lions immediately surrounded the reptile and played with it, patting its body and head. I have seen cobras move like lightning and I wouldn't have thought it possible for lions in such circumstances to survive without being bitten. My assistant's photographs, however, confirm his story. Finally the cobra made its getaway and the lions, their game finished, went peacefully to sleep.

Usually lions do not bother people, even if they have a chance. I had a young couple visit me in my camp at the Munge River. One day they decided to have a bathe in a nice secluded spot on the river, some thirty yards behind my camp. However, the young couple were not used to life in the wild. They had been bathing for over five minutes before they looked around them. There, no more than fifteen feet from them, lay a large black-maned lion, watching them with interest though no apparent hostility. Needless to say the young couple hastily streaked into my camp.

Young lions are very playful. This can be amusing but also at times dangerous. I once had three two-year-old lions try to play with me in my camp along the Munge River and I only managed to reach my car with some difficulty. It would have been a very one-sided game. I have frequently had two- or three-year-old lions make playful advances to the car and I am always doubly cautious if any of this age group are around.

I am also particularly on my guard when watching lions at night, for like hyenas their character changes during darkness. Many lions, which may be wary of people during daytime, become very bold at night. I shall never forget taking a visitor out for a night-time study of lions. This type of work is always done by moonlight since the lights of a car would disturb the animals. The lions we were watching were not used to cars but, as soon as darkness came, it almost seemed as if they considered my car as a supernumary member of their pride. At first they took no notice as we followed them over the moonlit plain. As they walked along they occasionally played briefly with each other. Then they began to make playful advances towards the car. I had to keep a close eye on them for I have no window on my side of the car, the driver's seat, so as to leave me plenty of room from which to photograph. When clouds obscured the moon for short periods, a lioness twice got close without my noticing, and so I decided it was too dangerous. I stopped the car, leaving the lions to continue on their own, and asked my visitor to pour me a cup of coffee whilst I made some notes. Suddenly I heard him whisper urgently: 'Hugo, look out!' Looking up, I saw a lioness on her hind-legs, her front legs draped over the bonnet of the car as she looked at us inquisitively. I started the engine and she left us in peace.

Leopards

In general leopards are solitary creatures. They usually live alone, except in the case of a mother and her cubs, and even this relationship apparently only lasts until the cubs are two or three years old, at which time they go their own way. When I began to study leopards I was told that it would be impossible to follow any individual, day-in, day-out. However, I found a couple, a mother and her two-year-old son of about the same size as herself, and discovered that, after some initial difficulties, I was able to observe them daily, even though at times I had to search for five or six hours first. As time went by I got to know the limits of their territory and noted there were certain trees they apparently preferred to rest in. So, gradually, it became easier to find them.

Female leopards have territories which they will defend from neighbouring females. Since almost all my observations were made on females and their cubs, I do not know much about the males. It appears they can move through the territories of various females but whether they have territories of their own is still a mystery. I have never seen an adult male and female together and suspect they tend to avoid each other except during courtship.

The usual size of a litter is two and, when a female has young cubs, she hides them, as a lioness would, for the first four weeks of their life. This might be in a cave, amongst rocks or in thick vegetation. Subsequently the cubs may spend much of their time in trees, where they will be somewhat more visible, though due to their superb camouflage they are rarely easy to see. Like lionesses, the female leopard when hunting will leave her cubs on their own, but when she has made a kill, she will collect her cubs and lead them to it.

The bond between a mother and her cubs is strong, and is expressed by their frequently playing together and licking each other. On the other hand the solitary nature of the leopard is shown when they rest, for they tend to remain apart, quite unlike lions which will often lie close together. Even more than lions, leopards spend most of their time resting, which meant that I spent most of my time watching sleeping leopards. Yet I was lucky, for I was at least watching *two* leopards, a mother and her almost full-grown son, and so there were some interactions and thus more activity than if I had been watching a lone individual.

To watch leopards was anyway a delight, for when they *did* move it was always stealthily and with a mysterious beauty. There was also the added satisfaction that little is known about their behaviour, and so there was the excitement of feeling a sense of discovery over almost everything I saw.

I well recall one day, for instance, when the young male leopard was in playful mood. It started when he climbed down from a tree which contained large sausage-shaped fruits. As he brushed forcefully past one of the fruits, his thigh bumped against it and it swayed away from him. When it swung back a second later, the fruit thumped him on the bottom. The leopard jerked around and growled at it, then swiped the sausage with one paw. The fruit swayed back and forth, violently at first, but then more gently. The leopard hit it again. Then he turned and continued his descent, occasionally patting at fruits as he did so. When he reached the ground, he looked around. Suddenly he flexed his legs and crept through the short grass, then pounced on to a dead branch, landing on one end. The branch bounced back at him but the leopard jumped aside and, as it passed him, attacked it from the rear, pinning it to the ground with both front paws and sinking his teeth into the soft wood. The branch stopped moving and the leopard left it, walking along beside a small stream. His step was jaunty and every now and then he patted at bits of vegetation.

Suddenly he froze in mid-step. A little way ahead of him was a warthog, grazing peacefully and completely unaware of his presence. Slowly the leopard sank until his tummy was almost touching the ground, then he stealthily crept forward through the high grass. His movements were so expert that, even though his body pushed the vegetation aside, the slow parting of the grass was almost unnoticeable.

When the leopard reached the edge of the high grass, the warthog, a large male, had its back to him. It was only a few yards off so the leopard had no trouble jumping on to its back. The warthog gave a snort of surprise and then pirouetted. To my surprise the leopard jumped off the warthog's back and bounded away after a butterfly. Almost as surprising, the warthog gave another snort and then calmly continued to graze.

One of the more tantalizing things about watching animals is that, unless you are exceptionally lucky, you can only concentrate on one of them at a time. I would have dearly liked to spend more time with this warthog, whose remarkable *sang froid* I much admired, but my responsibility was to the leopard. My virtue was rewarded, for a little further on the leopard crept up on a full-grown male giraffe. I wondered if he would dare jump on that but the giraffe saw him when he was still five yards away. After staring with big, brown eyes bordered by long lashes at the leopard below, the giraffe ran off.

Once again the leopard continued on his way. He had only gone another thirty yards, however, when he again sank on all four legs and crept forward cautiously. A moment later another leopard appeared from behind a bush. As the two-year-old pounced on it, it gave a growl of surprise and the two rolled on to the ground. Then they lay and licked each other. Belatedly I realized that this was not a territorial battle but that mother and child were happily re-united.

One day I was watching the mother leopard and her son as they rested in the shade of a bush beside a small stream. A troop of baboons was foraging on the short grass of the plains about a hundred yards upstream. Suddenly I saw one of the male baboons run forward and catch an infant Thomson Gazelle which had been lying hidden in the grass. There was some excitement in the baboon troop and, at the noise, the male leopard sat up and looked over the high grass which grew near the bush. Seeing the baboon carrying the infant gazelle, the leopard stood upright on his hind-legs. He watched keenly while the baboon headed for a tree which stood next to the stream, soon followed by the rest of his troop. There the baboon started to eat the gazelle.

Moving quickly but silently the leopard crept upstream towards them. When he was fifteen yards from the baboons he stealthily crossed a small, open patch and reached some thick bushes which led right up to the tree in which most of the baboon troop sat. On the ground at the base of the tree, a number of infant baboons played. I waited tensely, my finger on the camera button. I was still waiting tensely forty-five minutes later. Maybe, I thought, the leopard was waiting for some of the baboons to leave, for these powerful monkeys could be formidable enemies.

After an hour, the baboons did start to leave, until finally only the male remained, calmly eating the last bits of the gazelle. Now surely the action would begin. He finished his meal when the troop was a hundred yards away and without any haste descended the tree. I gently pushed the camera button until I felt resistance – a millimetre further and I would take a picture. As the baboon paused under the tree and picked up a scrap of meat he had dropped, I barely breathed. Then he walked in the opposite direction to the baboon troop, entering the bushes in which I knew the leopard was hiding. To my amazement, a few seconds later he emerged on the other side and walked along the stream. Yet I knew the male leopard was still in the bushes. The baboon must have passed within five yards of him. In walking downstream, the baboon was now walking straight towards the bush where the mother leopard lay. When he was ten yards from it he stood on his hind-legs, looked at the leopard for fifteen seconds or so, then calmly turned and followed his troop. He must have known the leopards were there all the time.

On another occasion I saw a troop of baboons playing in a tree with a leopard above them. It was inconceivable that they had not seen him yet they paid no attention. When they were forty yards away, the leopard descended the tree. At this, one of the male baboons at the rear of the troop immediately turned back and, on his own, chased the leopard away.

These and similar observations make me very sceptical of the general belief that baboons are a common prey of leopards. I am not saying that leopards never hunt baboons, for I believe leopards are opportunists and will hunt almost anything they can tackle. However, baboons usually move around in large troops and the males are exceedingly powerful creatures with canine teeth almost as large as those of a leopard. In the wild, a leopard cannot afford to get hurt, for, being solitary in its habits, it must rely on its own resources. A hurt leopard, if it cannot hunt, is likely to die of starvation unless it can keep itself going by scavenging, and in this it is at a disadvantage, for at kills it must make way for lions and hyenas. Thus I believe a leopard is above all concerned not to get hurt.

I remember watching the female and her cub as they rested in a tree when a pride of 22 lions passed. In addition to the adults the pride contained three tiny cubs only four weeks old and as they passed the tree in which the leopards lay, the mother leopard kept a close eye on them. The lion pride had only gone fifty yards when they saw some zebras and started to stalk them. The mother lioness took her cubs to an area of thick shrub about twelve yards square and, hiding them there, quickly joined the others in their hunt. The female leopard silently got up and descended her tree, walking cautiously towards the shrub in which the lion cubs were hidden. In the meantime, the zebras had noticed the lions and fled. The pride of 22 lay down only fifty yards from the shrubs, some resting, whilst others played with each other. This did not deter the leopard from continuing towards the shrubs but she moved more cautiously than I had ever seen a leopard do before, stopping every few feet to stare at the adult lions.

This she was able to do as long as she was in the open. However, once she disappeared into the thick shrub, I knew she would not notice if one of the lions decided to return to the cubs. I also knew that, if one of the cubs made a sound of distress, the whole pride would be with them in no time at all. Perhaps fortunately for the leopard, the cubs made no sound. Although the leopard zig-zagged silently through the shrubs for fifteen minutes, she never found them.

Lion cubs are not the only cats hunted by leopards. Twice I found the mother leopard eating a serval, and Miles Turner, for many years the Chief Park Warden of the Serengeti, told me he saw a leopard stalk and catch one of these cats. It was an amazing feat, for servals, with their large ears, have an acute sense of hearing. I think the only East African cat which I have never seen either being hunted or eaten by a leopard is the caracal, the African Lynx. This, however, is probably because the caracal is a rare and shy creature. I have no doubt that leopards would take them given the chance.

One morning I was following the mother leopard who was obviously hunting, when suddenly a small creature bounded away in front of her. I immediately recognized it as a hare and, as the leopard pursued it, swung around my camera to get a picture. However, I was thrown off course when the hare uncharacteristically rushed up a tree, closely followed by the leopard. It was only then that I realized it wasn't a hare, it was a wild cat. The leopard caught it in the crutch of two branches, grabbing it by the throat. The cat briefly clawed at the leopard's nose, but soon lay limp.

Of all the predators I have watched, the leopard seems the most calculating in its methods. I have frequently seen leopards watch a female gazelle for long periods, waiting for her to give away where her fawn lies hidden by going up to it in order to let it suckle. Once the leopard knows where the fawn is, it rushes forward. Normally in such circumstances the mother gazelle runs away, whilst her fawn reacts by hiding again, pressing itself close to the ground and remaining motionless. The leopard slows down, calmly walks up to the fawn and only takes the trouble to hurry if the youngster makes a last-minute attempt to escape.

I once found the mother leopard zig-zagging over a small area. My first thought was that she knew that an infant gazelle was hidden there; however, when she continued to zig-zag for more than half an hour, I became puzzled. It seemed to me she had covered every square foot, yet still she went on for another thirty minutes. Then she picked up an infant Grant's Gazelle. The incident showed both how well camouflaged these fawns were and how persistent a leopard could be in its hunting.

Normally a leopard will take its kill up a tree where it is safe from other predators, including vultures, for whilst these birds are quick to approach a carcass on the ground, they avoid those hanging in trees. However, kills are not always safe, even when deposited in a tree. One afternoon I watched as the mother leopard caught a Thomson Gazelle which she carried with some difficulty up a large tree. Once she lost her grip on its throat and it fell to the ground. When she carried it up again it got stuck between two branches, but finally she managed to tug it free and hung it over the fork of two large branches.

For a while, the leopard stood over the kill, panting, then she moved away from it and rested on another branch for fifteen minutes. When she had regained her strength, she climbed down the tree to collect her son whom she had left two hours earlier a mile from where she had successfully caught the gazelle. Whilst she was away nothing happened, and when the two leopards returned they fed in peace. When they had eaten much of the carcass was still left, enough to provide them with food for at least another day. For a while mother and cub licked each other, then both sought comfortable boughs on which to rest.

No sooner had they closed their eyes than a small head with beady eyes appeared from a hollow in the tree and looked around. A moment later a black-tailed mongoose emerged, went up to the kill and started to feed. A few yards away, the mother leopard was sleeping, then she suddenly opened her eyes and jumped forward at the mongoose with a loud growl. The mongoose shot back into the hollow with lightning speed. The mother leopard made herself comfortable again, but she had barely closed her eyes before the mongoose calmly emerged from its hollow and continued to feed. Again the leopard jumped at it and again the mongoose fled, only to return the moment the leopard had closed her eyes. That afternoon the leopard, joined later by her cub, was kept remarkably busy as bite by bite the mongoose got its full meal.

I saw another interesting behaviour pattern later that day. Moving through the tree, the female leopard occasionally bit off small, dead branches and dropped them to the ground. I saw her do the same thing on many occasions. Wild chimpanzees do the same. This is apparently a safety measure, guarding against the possibility that the animal might return, not notice the brittle branch, and step on it, thus crashing to the ground below. I have seen lions do something similar. They will carefully pick up branches with thorns which lie on an animal track and deposit them beside where they have been walking.

Some trees have so many long thorns that one would think it impossible for a leopard to climb them, yet I saw the mother leopard carry a gazelle up just such a tree. Although she moved very slowly and cautiously, I still couldn't understand how it was possible. There just didn't seem to be enough space between the thorns for her to put her paws. When she squeezed between two branches I was even more amazed that she didn't get any stuck into her. She repeated the remarkable performance during her descent, climbing down the tree head-first. Then she leapt to the ground, ironically straight on to a thorn hidden in the grass. She limped away from the tree, extracted the thorn with her teeth and went on to collect her cub.

Some prey are too big to be taken into a tree. I once found the mother leopard and her cub with a yearling wildebeest. The mother removed the stomach, which she carried some thirty yards away and partly covered with soil. Then, when she and the cub had fed, she bent a five-foot tree over the rest of the carcass, breaking the tree at its base. Later I was to see how effective this simple camouflage could be. The vultures found the stomach, which had not been well covered, but they did not see the wildebeest carcass only thirty yards away.

Two days later both leopards were up a tree in the same area. The mother had just caught a wildebeest calf which hung, uneaten, near them. There were no other wildebeest visible and I suspected the calf had been an orphan wandering alone in search of its mother. However, soon afterwards, a female wildebeest with a one-year-old offspring came running over the hill, calling loudly. As she ran back and forth for the next half hour, calling all the time, I realized she must be the mother. She seemed convinced that her calf must be in the area. I doubted if she had seen the kill, because whilst a mother wildebeest may attempt to save her calf when it is being attacked, she gives up when it is dead. It was pathetic to see her search so diligently. Finally she seemed to tire. Followed by her yearling offspring, she stopped running and, still calling from time to time, slowly walked straight towards the tree from which the two leopards were watching her closely.

As the mother wildebeest and her yearling walked along, they never looked up and the two leopards got ready to pounce on the yearling. Suddenly the mother wildebeest stopped, her yearling at her side, and looked round. They were only ten yards from the tree. The leopards remained motionless, waiting for them to come closer. However, the mother wildebeest turned and, followed by her yearling, disappeared over the hill and on to the open plain beyond, still calling for the calf and never realizing she had nearly lost two offspring that day.

Whilst leopards normally live and hunt in areas containing bushes and trees, this mother leopard also occasionally made long forays on to the open plains. One such expedition lasted for three days. Her cub never followed her on such trips but remained in a tree. With no trees available to the mother on the plain, she would rest underground in a den or burrow – whether for coolness or safety I do not know, probably both. A leopard is vulnerable on the plains, not only to lions but undoubtedly also to hyenas. I have never seen hyenas actually attack a leopard, but I have seen them steal a leopard's prey on a number of occasions before the cats could take their kills into the safety of a tree. In each case the leopard offered no resistance.

The leopard's enemies and prey are often alerted to the cat's whereabouts by the calls of Silverback Jackals. A family of these jackals may follow a leopard for a mile or more, uttering their shrill calls non-stop. Thanks to these calls, I often found leopards or knew there was one passing my camp at night. Strangely, guinea fowl will do the same. I shall never forget following the mother leopard across a plain when five guinea fowl noticed her. They immediately uttered their alarm calls and, running up behind her, followed in a row, calling all the time. In response to their sounds, other guinea fowl appeared and, running as fast as their short legs could take them, joined the queue until there were thirty of them following the leopard. From then on I was alert to the alarm calls of guinea fowl and often found leopards because of them.

Although sometimes difficult, it was not impossible to find the mother leopard and her nearly full-grown son almost daily. This was because her territory was fairly small, about one mile wide and five miles long, and did not contain a vast amount of thick vegetation. It seemed that her neighbour had a territory roughly similar in size but I did not attempt to study her in detail because her area did contain much thick bush. She also had a two-year-old cub, in this case a female. I twice saw the neighbours meet each other but, as the outcome was similar in both cases, I shall only describe one of them.

I was following the mother leopard and her son at midday along a stream, the banks of which contained a small strip of trees and bushes, when she reached the boundary of her territory. She stopped and stared. About one hundred yards into the neighbouring territory I could see a small herd of Thomson Gazelles grazing on the open plain. It was obvious that the mother leopard intended to hunt them and the cub climbed a tree and watched as his mother crept forward. It took an hour for the mother leopard to get close to her prey but then, for no apparent reason, the gazelles moved away across the plain. Slowly the mother leopard walked back to the small strip of trees, walking along its edge, back towards her own territory one hundred yards further up-stream. When she had gone thirty yards, she stopped and sniffed the ground for a while, then continued as if she were following a spoor. She was too pre-occupied to see the two leopards staring at her from a tree. When she passed them, the neighbouring mother silently descended and followed her. The mother leopard did not notice her neighbour until she had almost reached her. As the mother leopard fled, her neighbour ran parallel to her. Then, apparently on purpose, they ran smack into each other with their shoulders, both being thrown on to their sides on the ground. For a second they lay still, then the mother leopard fled again, once more pursued by her neighbour. This time the neighbour pounced on her bottom; the mother leopard briefly rolled over and fled into her own territory. The neighbour did not pursue her but climbed a tree and lay facing the mother leopard's territory. Soon afterwards, the mother leopard also climbed a tree and lay facing her neighbour forty yards away across the border.

The fight they had had was interesting in that both females had deliberately avoided hurting each other. It was symbolic rather than real and seemed to confirm my belief that it was of extreme importance for leopards not to get hurt. In facing each other from their respective trees, calmly, with no overt threats, the two females appeared to be reminding one another of the position of their borders. However, as they did so the male cub crept into the neighbour's territory where he pounced on the neighbour's daughter. From then on, for the rest of the afternoon, the two cubs played whilst above them their mothers confronted each other. Maybe the two cubs met each other more often after that. In any case, two years later the neighbour's daughter gave birth to twins.

Through the years I have got to know a number of leopards, although not so well as this mother and her cub. Each individual is recognizable by its spots and so, whenever I see a lady with a leopard skin coat, I can't help peering at it to see if I knew the leopard. I am also curious to know if the skin has any flaws. If not I wonder if it came from a certain dealer in Nairobi, who was seen to kill a leopard by holding it immobile in a crushcage, a cage the sides of which can be moved inwards, and then sticking a red hot poker up its anus.

Undoubtedly the leopard is one of the most graceful and beautiful of creatures. Transferring its coat to a lady does not necessarily make that lady either graceful or beautiful. On the contrary, it tends to do the opposite.

Cheetahs

I have watched cheetahs full time for about two months and have made incidental observations on them all my time in the Serengeti. This is, however, far less than in the case of the other animals I describe and I confess that I find them particularly perplexing in their habits and behaviour.

Like lions and leopards, cheetahs hide their cubs for the first four weeks or so of their lives. The usual litter is four but it is not uncommon to see a mother with five or six cubs. When cheetah cubs are about eighteen months old and the size of their mother, they separate from her; a move which I suspect is initiated by the mother. Judging by two brothers whom I have studied and by others I have seen, male siblings tend to remain together whilst females will become solitary. Again judging by these brothers, some males at least have their own territories. Whether females have territories I do not know; I suspect they might have, at least when they have young cubs.

The question of territoriality in cheetahs is complicated by the fact that they may travel vast distances as they follow the migration of their prey. Thus, while my brothers remained in their territory west of Lake Ndutu, at least throughout the rainy season, many other cheetahs also used this area for varying lengths of time, before either moving on of their own accord, or being chased out by the brothers. Although the brothers drove away both males and females their subsequent behaviour differed, depending on which sex they had chased. If a female, they would continue with whatever they had been doing before, usually resting. If a male, however, they would subsequently patrol that part of their territory, frequently marking trees with urine which they squirted at the trunk.

I remember one occasion when a female cheetah was hunting in the brothers' territory. As she crept up on a lone Grant's Gazelle, she in turn was being stalked. About one hundred yards behind her the two brothers had silently emerged from the marsh. It was not an easy hunt, for it took place over open ground and so the female had to concentrate fully on the gazelle's behaviour, moving forward when it grazed, freezing when it looked up. The brothers acted likewise but, being less concerned whether the gazelle saw them, made faster progress. As a result the gazelle ultimately did see them and bounded away. By the time the female cheetah looked around, the two brothers were running at her. She jumped into the air and fled, soon reaching a speed of 60 m.p.h. or more. Followed by the brothers, she reached the bush country where she disappeared amongst the thick vegetation. For the next half hour the brothers searched for her but finally they gave up and lay down, licking each other's faces.

I had watched similar incidents before and they puzzled me. I could understand the brothers chasing other males from their territory, but why a female? Maybe the competition for food, scarce in this area during the dry season, had something to do with it.

When I visited the Serengeti for the first time, I had been puzzled to see a female cheetah on the open plains approach a herd of Thomson Gazelles. She made no attempt to creep up on them and, when she did chase the herd, her pursuit seemed half-hearted. She didn't run at anything like full-speed. I wondered if she was ill. Subsequently she rested for half an hour and then repeated her performance with another herd of gazelles, again lying down to rest afterwards. She got up about fifteen minutes later and walked away, but when she had gone about sixty yards she suddenly rushed forward and grabbed an infant gazelle which had been lying hidden on the ground. When I saw her repeat these actions regularly over the next few days, I realized it was a hunting technique. When she ran openly at the gazelles, any fawns in the herd were likely to react by lying pressed to the ground. If she had merely walked towards them, the fawns might well have followed their mothers. Having thus forced the fawns to lie down, the cheetah would calmly wait until one of them made the mistake of raising its head and thus gave away its whereabouts. When the brothers hunted I often noticed a somewhat similar technique. Every thirty yards or so they would lie down as if in need of a rest. Perhaps they were, but they were also superbly well camouflaged and could keep an eye open on their surroundings, not only for small creatures such as hares, but also for gazelles wandering through the bush country.

It is said that a cheetah, the fastest land mammal, can run at a speed of 70 m.p.h. but only for a short distance. I have never timed one, but I do not doubt the assertion, for I have clocked Thomson Gazelles at 45 m.p.h. The gazelle, however, can keep this up for some distance and so it is obvious that the cheetah must catch up with its prey quickly. To do this, the cheetah first stalks the prey like a leopard, then when close enough begins to run, preferably when the prey isn't looking. Once the prey starts to flee the cheetah increases its speed. Soon it is going as fast as it can. When it has caught up with its prey, most usually a Thomson Gazelle, the cheetah throws it off balance by swiping at its hind-legs or rump with one paw. This is quite a feat, when one keeps in mind that one animal is running at 40 m.p.h. and the other probably a lot faster. Once the prey is caught, the cheetah usually kills it by biting into the throat. If tackling slower prey, such as a wildebeest calf, the cheetah may jump on to the back or rump of the victim, subsequently pulling it down to the ground.

When I suggested in 1961 that cheetahs might tackle surprisingly large animals, such as a full-grown zebra, I was considered crazy. I had reached this conclusion while making a film on Louis and Mary Leakey's research work at the Olduvai gorge where cheetahs were then abundant. Driving in bush country one day I came across five of them with a dead zebra. Unfortunately these cheetahs were timid individuals and immediately fled, soon disappearing from sight. I got out of my car and inspected the zebra. It was intact and still warm, with toothmarks on its throat. I felt this was reasonable evidence that it had been killed by the cheetahs. Since then a number of people have seen cheetahs kill fully adult zebras, wildebeests and kongonis, and it is now an accepted fact that they will tackle large prey.

I have never seen any of the carnivores except cheetahs go out of their way to teach their young to hunt. A mother cheetah will take a young gazelle alive to her cubs and let them play with it, quickly rushing to their aid if it should try to escape. She will also catch a wildebeest calf and hold it until her cubs join her, after which she may leave it to her cubs to finish off.

The most extraordinary lesson I ever saw of this kind involved a mother cheetah and her five half-grown cubs. With the mother in front and the cubs spread out behind her, they crept over the short grass plains towards a lone male Thomson Gazelle which was peacefully grazing about two hundred yards ahead. When the gazelle suddenly looked up, the mother cheetah immediately froze, but the cubs were a bit slow in following her example. I couldn't help laughing, for each froze in turn, one almost bumping into its sibling. They must have been very obvious, yet the gazelle continued grazing. Almost immediately, however, it looked up again and caught the cheetahs in mid-stride. Again the cubs froze in their haphazard way. The gazelle stared in their direction, then once more continued feeding. The cheetahs were too far away to be a threat and so the gazelle was not worried. In fact it seemed almost to make a game of catching the cheetahs out – sometimes even turning its back, only suddenly to look round. As the cheetahs advanced over the next hundred yards or so the scene was repeated time and time again, then the gazelle calmly walked away, its tail wagging jauntily.

Things are quite different when a mother cheetah with her cubs is hunting seriously. In some way which I have never discovered, the mother signals to the cubs to remain behind whilst she continues on her own. Once she has made the kill, she will either carry or drag it to the cubs. Cheetahs can be driven from their kills by any of the other carnivores described in this book except jackals. I have even once seen vultures in large numbers take over a kill from cheetahs, though normally the cats would chase these birds from the vicinity. I have never seen a cheetah scavenge, in the sense of eating something it has not killed itself, so it may well be one of the only carnivores, if not the only one, which does not do so or at least does so very rarely. Partly as a result of this it is probably less adaptable to a changing environment and thus more vulnerable in areas where man exterminates the prey animals.

Cheetahs have rarely been seen to mate and so I had always hoped to come across their courting. One day it looked as if I was lucky. I found four cheetahs together and one, the darkest of the group, was mounting one of the others. At this the two remaining ones attacked him. I quickly grabbed my camera and started taking pictures. Repeatedly the dark one tried to mount the female and as repeatedly the other two attacked him. At first I thought the three males were competing, but then I noticed that the other two males never tried to mount the female. I also saw that they and the female were all light coloured and so guessed they were siblings. Obviously the brothers were keeping a suitor at bay. Assuming I might not find them the next day, for cheetahs can be difficult to find, I took as many pictures as possible of this unusual behaviour.

It was barely light next morning when I set out to try to find the courting cheetahs again. I was lucky. They had barely moved and were still at it. It was too early to take pictures and so I concentrated on observing. That was when I discovered they were all males. Apparently it is not uncommon for young adult males to show homosexual behaviour. Some hours later a fully adult female joined them. As I followed them over the next few days, I realized I was watching a mother and her four almost full-grown sons.

One day the two brothers from the west of Lake Ndutu found this large family. It was five against two, yet the family fled – the mother pursued by one of the brothers whilst the other confronted the four males. In spite of their superior numbers the young cheetahs tried to run away; however, when one of them was attacked by the lone brother, the others stopped and watched, uttering pathetic bird-like calls. During the following ten minutes the brother repeatedly attacked one of the four. Twice he almost left, only to turn back instantly if one of the younger males moved. Gradually it became clear that, as long as they remained still, indicating submission, they were safe from attack. Finally none of them did move and the brother walked away. When he had disappeared from sight the four siblings fled in the opposite direction, meeting up with their mother the next day. They left the area shortly afterwards. The brothers were re-united an hour after the attack. They spent some time licking each other, then moved around their territory, marking trees as they did so.

Hyenas

There had been border incidents over the past two days in the north which had resulted in one dead and various wounded. It rained heavily most of the day, but when it stopped twenty individuals set out to patrol the threatened border. Earlier that year, when they had been fully engaged with incidents on their southern border, they had lost some ground in the north. When they reached the first spot which marked the border all seemed peaceful, but a little later they walked around a small hill and surprised fifteen of the enemy – members of the Scratching Rocks Clan. With roars and whoops, the hyenas of the Lake Side Clan charged and the enemy fled, uttering loud calls of alarm. In response to the sounds, reinforcements for both sides rushed to the scene so that ultimately there were eighty or more hyenas in the area. The Lake Side Clan were superior in numbers and, their tails held erect like banners, charged their enemies. For a moment the Scratching Rocks Clan held their ground, but when the others were almost upon them they turned and fled. The Lake Side Clan pursued them across the border, but they had only gone a short distance before the Scratching Rocks Clan wheeled around and attacked. Now the Lake Side Clan turned and fled, pursued back into their own territory until they in turn wheeled around and attacked. So it went on for the next half hour, each clan in turn chasing the other back across the border.

This is normal hyena warfare. Usually there is no physical contact, merely a chasing back and forth. It seems that hyenas are aggressive and bold when they see others within their own area but lose this boldness as soon as they find themselves in 'strange' territory. Nevertheless there are occasions in which hyenas are maimed or killed in this kind of warfare. In one year that I spent observing them in the Ngorongoro Crater I am certain more hyenas died fighting their own kind than from any other cause.

Within the one hundred square miles of the Crater floor, there are a number of hyena clans, but I mainly watched three; the Lake Side Clan, which has a territory on the North West of the Crater Lake, the Scratching Rocks Clan, which has their territory to the north of them, and the latter's neighbours, the Munge River Clan, which as the name implies, has a territory along part of the Munge River. In fact all three clans use this river, for it flows through all three territories on its way to the lake.

Hyena clans in Ngorongoro may consist of up to one hundred individuals or more, which share the same territory. As with lions, the females appear to be related, but the adult males were born in other clans. Unlike lions, however, it does not seem that young males are driven out of their original group; they leave of their own accord. Again like lions, each individual can wander around on its own or join up with any other member of its group. Females with cubs will tend to group together, although this tendency seems less strong than in lionesses. A peculiarity of hyenas is that females are larger than males and dominant to them; another, that the female's sexual parts look so similar to those of the male that it is impossible to distinguish them until a female has given birth and has teats.

Most of the hyena's activity takes place at night, including border patrols. The border is marked by the hyena rubbing a glandular secretion situated under its tail on to a piece of grass. Usually, prominent tufts of grass easily discernible in the countryside are used for such marking. The borders are exact and two adjoining clans will put their scent on the same tuft of grass, of course at different times. I once checked up on such a tuft of grass every evening for a week. First the Scratching Rocks Clan would arrive and mark it, then, often within half an hour, the Munge River Clan would appear and place their mark.

Normally hyenas respect each other's borders, except during a hunt when they will often pursue a prey into neighbouring territory. I remember following twenty members of the Scratching Rocks Clan one moonlit night. They were silent, except that one giggled briefly when another one nipped her bottom. Suddenly I noticed vague shapes in front of us – zebras. Almost immediately the hyenas gave chase and, changing gear quickly, I raced after them. Now the night air was filled with the braying of zebras and I could see several small herds quickly crowd together as they cantered across the plain. The hyenas had no trouble in catching up with the zebras but their attempts to separate a mare from the herd were repeatedly foiled by the stallions. As I watched, I saw a stallion turn and bite at a hyena, quickly twisting around afterwards and giving it a kick. The hyena rolled over in the dust but immediately got up and continued the chase. Now the stallion zig-zagged in front of the hyenas, occasionally kicking out or biting at one and in general slowing down the pursuit. Then he suddenly increased his speed and rejoined the herd.

The hyenas of the Scratching Rocks Clan continued the chase, encouraged by the sight of a zebra mare starting to lag behind. At some point in the chase they crossed the border into the territory of the Lake Side Clan. Soon afterwards the hyenas pulled the mare to the ground. Soon they were feeding noisily, each fighting the other as they scrambled for a share. Their sounds quickly attracted more members of the Scratching Rocks Clan, which nipped over the border to join the feast. Ultimately there were forty of them. Then suddenly there were many more and pandemonium followed. The Lake Side Clan had arrived and the Scratching Rocks Clan hastily retreated into their own territory. Now the new arrivals, at one time united against their neighbours, in their turn fought amongst themselves for a share of the zebra's carcass. In the darkness it was difficult to see the details of what was happening but I noticed that ten of them had got hold of a large section of the carcass and were tugging at it from all directions. Suddenly I realized that it was not part of the zebra but one of the members of the Scratching Rocks Clan. When they let go of her, she was unconscious, her toes, ears and sexual parts torn off. Mercifully she died without regaining consciousness.

With the ever-present possibility of aggressive neighbours crossing the border, it is not surprising that a clan's females tend to have their dens with their cubs towards the centre of their territory. A mother hyena usually has no more than two cubs at a time but, since the various mothers in a clan often join up in the same complex, there may be as many as twenty youngsters together. Thus, like lions, they tend to form a nursery group. Unlike lions, though, a female will not allow any but her own cubs to suckle from her and, if a female dies in a border incident or for any other reason, her cubs will soon perish of starvation.

Unlike most other carnivores, hyena cubs are born in an advanced state of development. Their eyes are open, many of their teeth are fully erupted and they are able to pull themselves along by their front paws. In view of this one would expect them to continue developing fast and to become independent of their mothers at an early age, but this does not happen. Youngsters rely on their mother's milk for eighteen months or so, far longer than any of the other African carnivores. This is probably due to the extreme competition for food at kills where, as I described earlier, each hyena must fight for a share. It would be dangerous for cubs to get involved in this sort of struggle. Nevertheless some cubs do join in much earlier than others. These are the offspring of the dominant female who, as the mother feeds, can lie protected between her front legs and share in the kill.

Competition is part of a hyena's life and starts almost at birth, for young cubs will compete aggressively with one another for their mother's teats. As a result, one of the cubs will establish dominance over the other at a very early age. This in turn is likely to lead to the dominant cub being better fed and thus growing stronger and more robust than the subordinate one. The struggle for dominance amongst two siblings is their own affair and is not influenced by the mother, who will attempt to give equal attention to both cubs. I say *attempt*, because the dominant cub will often thwart her good intentions.

This relationship between cubs and their mother was clearly illustrated in the Lake Side Clan by two large youngsters, half the size of their mother, whom I affectionately named the Terrible Twins. I called them this because when they weren't suckling, they whined, and since the subordinate one was seldom allowed to suckle, it was usually whining. Few animals can be as tolerant as a mother hyena. I remember once following the Terrible Twins and their mother. As usual the twins seemed to have an unquenchable desire for milk, or at least contact with a nipple, and whined incessantly and loudly. Finally, their mother was able to stand it no longer and lay down on her side. The dominant twin made itself comfortable and started to suckle, but when the subordinate twin tried to join in, its sibling immediately threatened it.

While the dominant cub suckled to its heart's content, its twin watched from a distance, looking dejected. It hung its head low and its whines grew more and more frantic. Its mother got up and approached the youngster, lying down in front of it and lifting one of her hind legs as an invitation to suckle. However, the dominant cub had immediately followed its mother and, having once again threatened its subordinate twin, it took their mother's proffered nipple. During the following half hour the mother repeatedly got up and lay down in front of her subordinate cub; each time her dominant cub blocked access to her nipple and suckled on its own. Finally, however, having apparently quenched its thirst, it let its twin join in. Both suckled for a while in peace.

By now the sun was high in the sky and it was hot. The mother hyena got up and, leading the twins to a small lake, lay down in the cool water. For a moment there was silence; then both twins whined frantically, for their mother's nipples were under water. After a minute, their mother tried to accommodate them by lying sideways in the shallow water but, whichever way she turned, there was always one nipple submerged. Finally she got up and went to the shore. After this peace was renewed, for, apart from suckling, the cubs appeared to find reassurance and comfort in contact with the nipple.

When cubs are younger and live in a den things are quite different, for then they may be left for long periods on their own whilst their mother hunts. In the Ngorongoro Crater a mother usually visits her small cubs at least once a day, although I once saw cubs stuck down their den for three days because a lion and a lioness were mating in a leisurely manner at the entrance. According to Hans Kruuk, a member of the Serengeti Research Institute who studied hyenas, cubs on the Serengeti are regularly left on their own for days on end. Presumably this is because, unlike in Ngorongoro, on the Serengeti prey animals may be scarce at certain times of the year, and so a mother hyena will have to travel vast distances in search of food. How she manages to traverse the territory of other hyenas in safety I do not know. The population density is less than in Ngorongoro, which must make things easier.

Generally a mother hyena does not bring back food for her cubs, so that they depend entirely on her milk. This is not surprising if one considers the large distance she may have to travel and the trouble she may have in competing with others for a share. Yet at times I have seen a mother return to the den with a bone or a skull, usually the last relic of a kill. At a den where there are many youngsters, she makes a great effort to ensure that her own offspring get the benefit of her prize.

Watching life around a hyena den can be great fun. The youngsters are extremely playful and surprisingly fast and agile, spending long periods chasing each other through the grass at top speed. They are also tough. It is not uncommon to see a cub so involved in its game that it forgets the lie of the land and suddenly disappears from sight as it tumbles down a den. No matter, within a second it rushes out again, covered in dust, continues the game, and runs smack into another cub which is standing around the corner, sniffing at a piece of grass. As the cubs play their mothers arrive, either singly or maybe two or three together. On their arrival the cubs briefly interrupt their games to greet them but, except for the offspring of the newly arrived female which settle down to suckle, they are soon chasing each other again.

The cubs of the Lake Side and Scratching Rocks Clans soon got used to my car. They often came up to sniff at it and ultimately even disappeared under the car during their games. The adult females too occasionally came up to have a look and it was at such times that their immense size became apparent. A female can weigh one hundred and ninety pounds or more and, standing on all fours, could poke her head into my Land Rover window. Since I have no glass in it, I had to be cautious, especially at night. One of the common fallacies about hyenas is that they are cowards and would not dare attack man. This is far from true. There have been many cases of individual hyenas, or hyenas in large groups, entering villages and attacking man. They are in fact tough creatures with incredibly powerful jaws, strong enough to pulverize a legbone.

Whilst hyenas can be active during the daytime, especially in the rainy season, their busiest time is night. I have often watched them by moonlight. One night I remember I was following a hyena of the Scratching Rocks Clan. Shortly after sunset it joined up with a group of eight other members of the clan. For an hour they patrolled their southern border, occasionally stopping to mark selected tufts of grass.

When an hour had passed, the individual I was following left the others and walked around on its own, occasionally sniffing at the grass. When it heard another hyena whooping in the distance it stopped and listened, then, pointing its nose to the ground, it whooped in response. It did not try to find the other hyena, however, but merely continued on its way. Finally it lay down and went to sleep. It was nine o'clock. At two o'clock it was still asleep, not having stirred for the past five hours. I waited patiently, drinking one cup of coffee after the other. Then, with startling suddenness, the hyena leapt to its feet and rushed off. I hastily threw the remnants of my tenth cup of coffee out of the window, started the car and raced after the hyena, which was only vaguely visible in the darkness ahead of me. When I caught up, the hyena was standing still, listening. I switched off the car engine and strained my ears but could hear nothing unusual. Nor apparently could the hyena, for it lay down and went to sleep again. I poured myself another cup of coffee and, after half an hour, yet another, but I never took my eyes off the indistinct sleeping shape, for I knew that it might lead me to a hunt. If I didn't react quickly enough when it jumped up and ran, I would lose it in the dark.

It was four o'clock before the hyena jumped up again and raced away. I had started the car as it moved and now raced after it. As we approached Scratching Rocks Hill, I could see some other hyenas chasing a wildebeest on the crest of the hill. When the wildebeest reached the rocks, it put its rump protectively against a large boulder and faced its pursuers. The hyenas hesitated, but when one of them moved around the boulder, the wildebeest turned, exposing its rump to the others and thereby sealing its fate. Shortly afterwards its carcass was covered by forty hyenas, squabbling loudly with each other. It was a savage sight, made worse when suddenly two male lions jumped from behind the rocks amongst the hyenas, grabbing one of them. As the lion bit into the hyena's back, it screamed. The other hyenas had fled but now they turned and watched as the raider continued to maul their fellow clan member. Then the lion joined its companion on the wildebeest carcass and both fed. Behind them the wounded hyena sat pressed against a rock, its mouth wide open in a terrified gape as it screamed gratingly and loudly. It couldn't move, for its back had been broken. When one of the lions had fed for a while it slowly walked up to the terrified hyena, dragged it away from the rock and throttled it by biting into its throat. It gave an impression of viciousness such as I had never before seen in an animal. Since then I have seen male lions go out of their way to creep up on a hyena, yet they seem to have no object except to kill it. Certainly I have never seen lions eat one.

Whilst hyenas are dominated by adult lions, their relationship with adult lionesses can be quite different. This was clearly illustrated when the Munge River pride of lions killed a buffalo. By the time the hyenas discovered them most of the lions had fed and had gone to the river to drink. When only one lioness remained on the kill, the fifty hyenas moved in. The lioness left, but then suddenly turned and grabbed one of the hyenas by the neck, shaking it vigorously. Without hesitation the other hyenas attacked the lioness, biting at her rump. The lioness let go of her victim, which immediately turned and also attacked her. Snarling, the lioness fled, the victorious hyenas close on her heels, whooping loudly.

Such incidents with lionesses are not rare and belie the traditional belief that hyenas are cowards. Who would have believed some years ago that hyenas would attack a rhino calf with its mother there? Yet I have seen this happen a number of times. As is so often the case when smaller animals confront larger ones, the smaller ones are faster and so the hyenas can usually avoid a mother rhino. Not always, though; I once saw a rhino spear a hyena with its horn, lifting it off the ground and throwing it into the air.

Of course, like most carnivores, hyenas also scavenge and they are very aware of the movements of vultures which often indicate where a carcass lies. I have frequently seen hyenas run cross-country for five miles or more to where vultures were landing. Sometimes their journey was in vain; the birds were merely drinking, bathing, or on one occasion, catching flying ants no larger than mosquitoes. In this last case, the hyena never did work out what the birds were up to. As they flew from one colony of ants to another, the hyena rushed after them, each time looking puzzled to find the birds apparently eating air.

One day I was following a male of the Lake Side Clan when a shape crept through the high grass towards it. It was a Kori Bustard, a large bird but hardly a match for a hyena. However, much to my surprise, the bird suddenly fluffed out its feathers and approached in a threatening attitude. The hyena stopped and stared but slowly retreated when the bird got close. For a brief moment it turned and looked as if it was about to go for the bird but the Kori Bustard seemed fearless and the hyena hesitated, then fled.

The courage and intelligence of these birds is indeed remarkable. Some years ago I saw a pack of wild dogs come across a wounded Kori Bustard. The bird staggered away from them, one wing limp. The dogs immediately chased it and, with an obvious effort, the bird managed to fly a short distance, collapsing on the ground forty yards further on. As the dogs raced to the spot, the bustard again tried to run, staggering from side to side. Yet, when the dogs were almost upon it, the bird effortlessly took to the air. It had successfully led the dogs away from its nest and had completely fooled me too.

At the bottom of the Ngorongoro Crater there is a lake which contains soda water. It is an ideal feeding ground for flamingoes and when I was making a film there a few years ago there were a hundred thousand or more of these birds on the lake. There can be few sights so spectacular as thousands upon thousands of pink flamingoes and this becomes even more awe-inspiring when large clouds of them take to the air, drift over the lake for a short distance and then gracefully settle on the water again. The hyenas of the Lake Side Clan were one of the reasons for this phenomenon. When I first saw them run full-speed into the shallow lake I thought that they had been attracted by the sight of so many creatures but would never be able to catch any of them. I was wrong. To be able to take off, the flamingo has to run for a short distance, at first treading water but finally skimming along the surface until it gains the necessary momentum. With so many birds so close together, there was little room for manoeuvre and occasional mistakes occurred. The hyenas hunted flamingoes daily for many weeks and were quite often successful. Hunting was confined to males and young females; the fully adult females could not keep up the necessary speed when running in the lake. The drag of the water on their larger bodies was apparently too great. Instead they waited at the edge of the lake and stole a share from the others when they emerged. Of course, many flamingo hunts were not successful and I regularly saw males, running at full speed, suddenly disappear underwater and throw spray into the air as they encountered an unexpected deep spot.

Hyenas are at home in the water. For some reason, wildebeest often try to escape hyenas by running into the lake or the Munge River. This manoeuvre merely seals their fate. Hyenas can even feed underwater. I once saw the Scratching Rocks Clan kill a wildebeest in the Munge River at a spot where the water was about six feet deep. Soon the carcass sank under-water. From then on the hyenas felt for the carcass with their feet, then dived under-water, emerging a moment later with a large chunk of meat in their mouths. With their coats all wet, smooth and dark, they looked remarkably like a colony of seals.

Probably even more than is the case with any of the other African carnivores, the hyena is an opportunist, adaptable and able to eat a great variety of foods. I once found one trying to chew through the hard shell of a large tortoise. It didn't succeed, but the marks it left explained the scars I had seen on many other tortoises in the past. I don't doubt that, if the tortoise had been smaller, the hyena would have succeeded in making a meal of it.

Where hyenas live near human habitation they may become full-time scavengers, clearing up some of the rubbish of man. I once found a hyena stumbling through the bush, bumping into trees and rocks because it had a tin stuck over its head. Fortunately I was able to get some help and, as it was not a very large specimen, we were able to remove the tin. Like lions, hyenas often visit my camp at Ndutu, but unlike lions they take a keen interest in my tents, especially the kitchen and the dining tent. In fact, until I had a hyena-proof kitchen built, a number of my excellent meals were stolen.

Unfortunately, even today, with more knowledge and understanding available, most people dislike hyenas and look incredulous when I say I have a great affection for them. Yet I know that if these same people had the chance to watch them, as I have done, and to get to know individuals, they too would come to like them. The cubs are playful and humorous and can be quite beautiful at about one year old. The adults are affectionate to them and, though not endearing in appearance, have great character. Certainly they have some traits which make them unattractive to man, but then so do the other carnivores and so does man too as a species. I have always found that the more I get to know individual animals and humans, the more I understand and like them.

Jackals

I have, of course, seen jackals all over the Serengeti, but it is above all on the plains of the Ngorongoro Crater that I have watched them most intensively. Three species of jackal live there: the Golden, the Silverback and the Sidestripped. It is unusual to have these three species in the same area and habitat; the Golden Jackal more usually inhabits the open plains, whilst the Silverback and Side-stripped favour the bush country. At least this is the case in East Africa where the three species meet: the Golden Jackals extending north as far as Israel, the Silverbacks south to South Africa and the Sidestripped as far across as the west coast, where I saw them in Senegal.

Nothing much is known about Sidestripped Jackals. They have shorter ears than the other two species, and this is the feature which most clearly distinguishes them from the very similar Golden Jackals. Many individuals, but not all, also have a white stripe along their sides and again many, but not all, have a white tip to their tails.

Many people in the field find it equally difficult to distinguish on occasions between Golden and Silverback Jackals. This is because Golden Jackals vary widely in their colouring; not only do individuals differ, but each individual changes in colour throughout the seasons. Thus Golden Jackals may have a saddle which can be dark or more often silvery, though this seldom contrasts as sharply with the rest of their body as is the case with Silverbacks. Basically the colour of a Golden Jackal is fairly uniform, varying from grey, to sandy, to golden.

Golden Jackals live in pairs, possibly mating for life. Offspring may remain with the parents until they are fully adult and help look after the subsequent litter. A fairly small area around the den appears to be territorial and strange Golden Jackals entering it are normally attacked and driven away. A wider hunting range overlaps with that of the neighbours. Interactions between neighbours vary widely, from friendly behaviour to aggression, a difference in attitude which I suspect depends on whether or not the jackals are related.

The jackal's food is varied: fruit, mushrooms, insects, rodents, snakes, gazelles and carrion. However, the food which individual jackals eat is dependent on their habitat. Thus some jackals may never have eaten fruit and I have never seen jackals on the Serengeti eat snakes, although they may well do so on occasions. In the Ngorongoro Crater, on the other hand, I have frequently seen Golden Jackals eat snakes. Sometimes they pick up a snake by its back or tail, and eat it without troubling to kill it first; at other times they will fight it, grabbing it with a lightning movement, shaking it vigorously for a second and then letting it go before it has a chance to turn its head and retaliate. They repeat this manoeuvre a number of times until the snake is dead. From my observations it would seem that jackals know which snakes are dangerous and which harmless.

One of the most amusing incidents I witnessed with jackals concerned the eating of mushrooms. This took place in the Ngorongoro Crater when I was watching a family of two adults and four cubs. The whole family had been eating mushrooms of various types, but one day I saw one of the cubs eat a species I had not seen jackals eat before. Ten minutes later the cub seemed to go mad. He rushed around in circles and then, to my amazement, charged flat-out, first a Thomson Gazelle and then an adult wildebeest. Both animals stared at the tiny creature and hurried out of its way. Unfortunately I could not find another mushroom of that type for identification. I feel convinced the cub was suffering from hallucinations.

It is unfortunate that jackals are persecuted by farmers in many areas, for I suspect that, if proper research were done, it would be shown that they are often positively beneficial. Certainly in the Ngorongoro Crater the main food of the Golden Jackals is rodents and on the Serengeti the same is true of Silverback Jackals. Though there is no doubt that in some areas jackals will take fruit and livestock, I think they do this less often than they are normally accused of. Before deciding to get rid of the jackals, each farmer should take into account that, without them, the rodent and insect population on his farm is likely to increase considerably.

I remember vividly watching a pair of jackals one day on the Serengeti. Around me the open plain, stretching from one horizon to the other, was barren and dry except for one green patch a few square miles in size. The short rains had failed, but this spot had had two torrential downpours. From many miles away the Thomson Gazelles moved in to feed on the succulent grass and give birth to their young. Their fawns learnt to walk and run within fifteen minutes of being born, but, unlike wildebeest calves, they did not stay close to their mothers; most of the day they lay hidden, usually amongst the foot-high patches of sodom apple plants. Even from close by they looked like one of the small mounds of bare earth so common amongst these plants and they were almost as motionless, especially if one of the predators was nearby.

There were many predators in this green patch, but as far as I could determine, they were all residents – the hyenas and Golden Jackals which lived here all year round. They had had a long dry season to contend with during which prey had been scarce. Now the fortunes of weather had congregated hundreds of gazelles in their hunting grounds.

The jackal pair I was watching zig-zagged amongst the Thomson Gazelles, going from one patch of sodom apple plant to the next. Most of the gazelles took little notice, but every now and then a female would watch their progress intently, as if nervous lest they might find her fawn. Whether in fact this behaviour indicates the gazelle has a fawn hidden, I do not know; if so, the jackals had not learnt to take their cue from the adult's behaviour for they frequently by-passed such females, spending no more time in her area than elsewhere.

The two jackals did not always stay close together as they searched. There were many patches of vegetation to inspect and, even with two of them, they could not hope to cover more than a small section of their hunting range. Many fawns escaped detection that day. One was especially lucky. A female Thomson Gazelle had for some time been watching the approach of the jackals. When the male jackal headed towards an isolated patch of sodom apple plants in the short grass, she left the small herd of gazelles and followed him. By the time he reached his destination she was close on his heels. Suddenly a small form bounded away, no more than two feet in front of the predator. Without hesitation, the gazelle charged and the jackal only escaped her sharp horns by jumping sideways. With lightning movements the jackal zig-zagged in front of the gazelle, who persisted in her pursuit, then he abruptly turned and continued chasing his prey. Seconds later the female gazelle was again close on his heels and once more the jackal had to jump sideways in order to escape her. This time, the mother did not stop but, turning away from the jackal, ran fast after the small form bounding away in the opposite direction. Then suddenly she stopped and stared. The small form was now standing still and, balanced high on its hind-legs, stared back at her with long ears twitching. It was a hare. The gazelle turned and went back to the isolated patch of vegetation where she found her fawn still lying motionless.

I have seen this happen on two other occasions. Once I felt sure that, like me and the mother, the jackal thought he was chasing an infant gazelle. Normally jackals ignore hares even when they are only a few yards away, for they are difficult prey to catch. Not only are they fast long-distance runners, but if far enough ahead of a predator, they may suddenly hide, pressing themselves amongst some vegetation or dashing down a den.

Not all fawns were lucky that day. Soon afterwards one suddenly jumped up from under the female jackal's nose. As it leapt away, the jackal grabbed it by a hind-leg and it fell on to its side, struggling and squealing loudly as the jackal changed her grip to its belly. Suddenly its mother was there and it was free, struggling to its feet and bounding away as fast as its legs could take it whilst its mother chased the jackal in the opposite direction. It had escaped but not for long; whilst its mother pursued the female jackal, it was caught by the male.

Jackals are more successful in hunting Thomson fawns when they hunt in pairs. I have frequently seen lone jackals lose their prey because of the mother gazelle's attacks, but when two are involved, the scene described above is common. In some cases I had the impression that one jackal intentionally lured the mother away from its young. Not only are jackals fast runners, but they can take sharper corners than gazelles, and I have only twice seen one being hit. In neither case was the jackal wounded. On the other hand mortality among the fawns is high; I saw fifteen kills in one week.

Jackals normally kill prey, such as gazelles, by eating into the groin and stomach. This sounds gruesome and looks horrible, but in fact death usually occurs more quickly than under the system commonly used by cats, suffocation by holding on to the prey's throat. I have only twice seen a jackal suffocate its prey, in both cases gazelle fawns.

While the male jackal fed, his mate approached him submissively. He looked up and snarled at her, so she moved away and lay down. Most jackal pairs I have watched will share their kills, but in this case the male would normally not allow his mate to join him. When he had finished feeding, he picked up the remains of the kill and trotted off. The female immediately moved over to where he had fed and found some tiny scraps. In the meantime the male buried the remains some hundred yards further on. Later he would return for a second meal, but he would search in vain; when he disappeared from sight, the female dug up his larder and absconded with the remains.

Having buried the remains of his kill, the male jackal made his way across the green patch. His tummy was bulging and he no longer zig-zagged through the herds but walked in a straight line. After a while he reached a small hole in the ground and, poking his head down it, made some whining sounds. Then he hurriedly backed away as three small cubs dashed from the dark hole and pushed their noses to his mouth. He opened his mouth wide and regurgitated the fresh meat for them. The cubs ate slowly. They were only about four weeks old and had just started to eat meat, still depending primarily on their mother's milk. When she arrived fifteen minutes later, they rushed up to her and suckled greedily, standing upright on their wobbly hind-legs in order to reach her teats as she stood over them. Female jackals seldom lie down for their cubs to suckle.

Subsequently the cubs played briefly, biting gently at each other, but when a warm wind began to blow over the plains, they returned to the coolness of their den. The two adult jackals briefly groomed each other, nibbling gently at one another's faces and necks. Then, wandering a small distance from the cub's den, they too disappeared underground. I settled down in the car, prepared to wait for the jackals to reappear. It would probably not be for several hours, for the heat of midday was becoming intense. In the distance I could see where the hot wind blew over bare patches of ground beyond the patch of green; huge clouds of white dust were swept into the air and across the dry country.

Not till the setting sun had turned the country golden did the parent jackals call the cubs from the den. While the female suckled the youngsters, the male left to dig in vain for the remains of the gazelle which his mate had stolen earlier. Later one of the cubs found an infant Thomson Gazelle lying hidden in the grass. He pounced towards it and shook his head at it as an invitation to play. When the fawn did not respond, he shook his head again, but then the mother gazelle arrived and chased the jackal cub off.

No more rain fell on the green patch and after a week it looked no different to the surrounding country. Most of the gazelles moved elsewhere, their dainty hooves kicking up dust as they went. The jackals returned to hunting insects and the hyenas soon started to look lean again. I had twice seen hyenas eat jackal cubs so it did not surprise me when one day one of them poked his head down the jackal's den. As I watched, I heard the tiny yowl of a jackal cub in the den. Suddenly the hyena giggled hysterically, its protruding rump had received two vicious bites from the parent jackals. They had been sleeping nearby and, at the cub's yowl, had rushed to its defence. Moments later the hyena retreated, with both adult jackals nipping at its sensitive heels. Squatting, the hyena tried to cover its heels with its large bottom. It pirouetted as it tried to snap at its tormentors, but the jackals persisted in their attacks and finally the hyena scuffled along in a sitting position away from the den. When it had moved some fifteen yards the jackals stood and howled in unison. The hyena took the opportunity to run off in search of easier prey. It had got close to the cubs, but luckily they had been out of reach deep down in the den.

Next day the mother jackal moved her cubs to a new den whilst her mate watched her. This should have been a fairly straightforward operation, but the female seemed young and inexperienced. She had considerable trouble in picking up and carrying the cubs and they, for their part, seemed none too keen on the procedure. As the mother tried to get a grip on their fur, they desperately scrambled away from her until finally she carried them clumsily by whatever part of their body she could get hold of – paw, tail, neck or body.

Once established at the new den, both male and female set to work to excavate the entrance. Sometimes the two competed actively for this job, both trying to get down the entrance first. On one occasion the female vigorously pulled the male out of the den by his tail, for which impertinence she received a nip on her nose. When the first clouds of dust flew out of the den, the cubs, standing at a distance, watched inquisitively. They had never seen digging before and one of them rushed over to have a closer look, then suddenly recoiled as the dust flew into its face. From then on it kept at a safe distance.

Jackals regularly move their young cubs from one den to the other; sometimes only a hundred yards away, sometimes half a mile. I suspect this may be to avoid predators (and also for the sake of cleanliness). The smells around a used den may attract predators and, once its location is known, a predator such as the hyena that was chased away may return when the parent jackals are off hunting. Hyenas are not the only predators. Leopards take adult jackals and no doubt will take youngsters too if given the chance. But I think the greatest danger for cubs comes from the air in the shape of the martial eagle, a tiny speck in the sky until, folding its wings, it hurtles towards the earth. I remember once hearing the sound of wind streaking through feathers, seeing the sudden alarm of the jackal cubs, the talons reaching for one of them, digging moments later deep into flesh, and then the cub being swept up into the sky. The family I was now watching was lucky, for apart from the one incident with the hyena, I never saw them in danger.

The two adult jackals I was watching were alert to the movements of the vultures. If one of these folded its wings and headed towards the earth, then the jackals were up in a flash and running fast to where the bird was heading. Sometimes, if the carcass was close, they even arrived on the scene before the vultures, but usually by the time they got there numerous birds were already fighting for a share. Sometimes there were so many birds scrambling over the carcass and on top of the others, that it was impossible to see what dead animal lay beneath.

Vultures have sharp beaks and it seemed to depend on the degree of its hunger whether a Golden Jackal would be bold enough to move in on such a feast. If one did approach, it was with rounded back and mouth wide open, lips curled back in a snarl. But the jackals rarely used their teeth when attacking vultures; instead, on reaching the birds they would suddenly swing their body around in a powerful movement so that their rump slammed into the opposition. This system of fighting has the advantage that the jackal's face, with its sensitive nose and eyes, is turned away from its opponent and thus protected from a retaliatory attack. It is not only used against vultures, but also amongst jackals when determining their relative dominance. I have never seen an opponent seriously hurt by such attacks and it is thus an effective way of settling disputes without physical damage to either party.

Golden Jackals are less apt than Silverbacks to dart in amongst feeding vultures. Silverbacks seem more agile when attacking the birds with a body-slam during which all their feet may leave the ground. I have seen them do this with so much force that, on missing the fleeting bird, the jackal cartwheeled 360 degrees through the air. It is therefore surprising that Golden Jackals on the plains are normally dominant to Silverbacks. I remember following the two adult Golden Jackals one day as they were hunting. When they saw some vultures landing over a mile away, they quickened their pace, but they were not in a great hurry for they had eaten some hours earlier. When they arrived on the scene, three Silverback Jackals were eating from the carcass amidst a circle of vultures which watched them intently with necks outstretched and uttering grating sounds.

As the Golden Jackals came closer, the three Silverbacks showed signs of submission but continued to feed for as long as possible. Then two made their getaway but the third hesitated for too long and was attacked. It sank submissively to the ground, its ears back, while the two Golden Jackals in turn slammed their bodies against it. Then the Silverback tried to retreat, but the Goldens soon caught up and the Silverback again lay down submissively. Again the attacks were repeated until finally the Silverback managed to get away and join the other two some fifty yards from the kill. The Golden Jackals headed back to the carcass, but the vultures had made good use of the interlude and were squabbling amongst themselves. The Golden Jackals stopped and watched the scene but made no effort to share in the meal. For the vultures it was a lucky day because, for the next half hour whilst they fed, the Golden Jackals kept the Silverbacks at bay.

One morning I arrived at the jackal den to find it deserted but, scanning the surrounding countryside with binoculars, I saw the family trotting along the horizon, the two adults in front and the cubs following closely behind. By the time I reached them, there was confusion. There seemed to be jackals all over the place. It took me some time to sort out who was who and what was happening. In addition to the family I was studying, there were six other jackals, two adults and their four one-year-old offspring. In addition, this family had new-born cubs in a den in the area. To my surprise there was no aggression, even though my family was deep in its neighbour's territory and was almost on top of a den which contained new-born cubs. As the female moved towards the den, none of the other jackals tried to check her. Instead they stood and watched. Nor did any of them move when she reached the cubs' den and listened intently at the entrance, nor even when the new-born cubs could be heard whimpering in distress below the ground.

For five minutes or so the female and her nine-week-old cub sniffed around the den area. The neighbouring female watched intently, as did one of her yearlings, but the adult male had lain down and appeared to be asleep whilst the three other one-year-olds had moved away. Finally, the female jackal and her cub left the den. Approaching the other jackals, both she and her cub submissively greeted the adult male and the female. The greeting with the former was brief, but with the neighbouring female it was intense.

I have no scientific proof that these two families were related but in my own mind I am convinced that this was the case. The female I had been studying was young, probably two years old. The neighbouring adults, I believe, were her parents and she had probably helped them raise the subsequent litter, the four one-year-olds. Thus they all knew each other well, which would explain the lack of aggression shown towards an apparent intruder and also the tolerance extended towards her mate – though I noticed that he took no risk of out-staying his welcome but had moved off as soon as his female approached the neighbours' den. It was still more remarkable that, when one of the visiting nine-week-old cubs was threatened by one of the resident yearlings, it was the yearling's mother who came to the rescue; in other words, if my guess is right, the cub's grandmother was intervening to protect him from the bullying of his elder cousin.

But how can I explain the pattern of another den which I had watched a year earlier? Here there were two adults and four cubs; but two of the cubs were about eight weeks old and the others no more than four. Had the male bred by two mates and one of them died? It was possible, but I had never seen a male jackal with more than one mate. Or were two of the cubs the offspring of neighbours – perhaps related – whose parents had perished and who had been rescued and adopted by the adults I was watching? On the whole I subscribe to this view, but I will have to find out a great deal more about jackals before I say so with any confidence.

Wild dogs

African wild dogs are not domestic dogs that have gone wild; their ancestors were always wild and in fact they might well have been called African wolves, for in many ways the behaviour of the two species is similar. Like wolves, African wild dogs were despised by man and persecuted almost to extinction. This hatred was based, in both cases, on the many misconceptions which existed about their behaviour. So strongly were these held that when I started to study wild dogs I found it almost impossible to separate fact from fiction. The easiest thing seemed to be to ignore all I had ever read and start from scratch. At that stage I had only planned to do a six-month study, but I became so fascinated that the work ultimately stretched over many years.

One group of dogs, which I grew to know intimately, I called the Genghis pack. Because the typical pack leads a nomadic life, roaming ten miles a day or more over a territory of a thousand square miles, they can be extraordinarily difficult to follow. In time, however, I realized that the pack did have certain spots in which they preferred to rest during the heat of the day. I began to concentrate on these places; waterholes, for instance, or even a specific tree. The problem was still formidable, however, and it was not unusual for me to have to spend two or three weeks searching before finding the pack. Then it was a matter of remaining with them as long as possible, but I could rarely manage this for more than three or four days at a time and even then only if there was a moon so that I could follow the dogs at night. This was frustrating work and I was always delighted when a female was due to give birth and selected her den. At such a time she would often come into a false heat, an ingenious device which ensured that the pack would remain with her rather than continue their travels.

This device was the more effective because in the Genghis pack, as in most of the fifteen or so packs I have observed, there were many more males than females. The males were usually brothers, or at least litter-mates, who remained remarkably loyal to each other. Their sisters, however, were driven out by the dominant female, eventually to join up with other packs and thus reduce the risk of in-breeding. Once they were accepted into another pack one of them would become the dominant female and she would ultimately drive the other females away.

The wild dogs, like most animals which use burrows, prefer to take advantage of existing vacant ones rather than dig their own. The pregnant female spends a considerable time removing any roots which may have grown into an old den and she may also enlarge it. Subsequently she and the pack hunt within fifteen to twenty miles of the den, returning to it every two or three days. I presume these regular visits are to ensure no other animal establishes residence there.

Then one day, shortly before the female is due to give birth, she remains at the den and refuses to follow the pack when it sets off to hunt. This can cause confusion. When Havoc, dominant female of the Genghis pack, refused to follow, the other dogs hesitated to leave and appeared not to understand why she would not join them. Repeatedly they walked off a short distance, then waited for her, summoning her with calls of distress. She herself was clearly torn between a desire to join them and the need to stay, for she would follow them a short distance, then return to the den and in her turn utter calls of distress. Maybe the veteran male Yellow Peril, father or uncle to the other males of the pack, alone understood the situation, for when the pack did finally leave, he remained with Havoc and guarded her den as she gave birth.

For the first three to four weeks of their life, the puppies remain underground. A normal litter is ten, but on occasion I have seen as many as sixteen puppies. The mother dog spends most of her time during this period underground with her pups. Normally she does not join the rest of the pack on their hunts; instead, the other dogs feed her by regurgitating meat. Once the puppies emerge into daylight, they too are fed by regurgitation, at three weeks old. However, the mother's milk still forms an important part of the diet for another five weeks or so.

Complications arise when, as sometimes happens, two or more females remain within the pack and give birth at about the same time. In my book *Solo: The Story of an African Wild Dog* I tell how Havoc, the dominant female of the Genghis pack, stole and killed the puppies of the subordinate female. When, in the Pimpernel pack, two females gave birth, I wondered whether the same would happen. The three females in the Pimpernel pack were Spitfire and Soda, which were sisters, and an older female related to them, Gretel. Spitfire was the dominant female, with Soda second and Gretel the subordinate, even though she was older than the other two. Spitfire was the first to give birth. It was her first litter. Whether she timed it wrong or had other problems, I do not know, but in any case, she went down her den, but did not reappear. After three days had gone by, I wondered whether she had died. With Spitfire gone, Soda started to mark the surrounding area, a prerogative of the dominant female. On the third day, as she was doing this, she suddenly froze and stared at Spitfire's den as if seeing a ghost. Sure enough, there was the missing mother. Cringing, Soda quickly edged towards her mate and rubbed up against him, whilst still staring at Spitfire. However, Spitfire almost immediately disappeared underground again and, although acting somewhat nervously, Soda continued to behave as if she were the dominant female.

Four days later Spitfire again emerged from her den. This time she unexpectedly ran out at full speed on hearing the males return from a hunt. As she reached Soda, her sister immediately made submissive gestures and Spitfire briefly bit her neck, as if reinforcing her dominance. During the next few days, Soda still occasionally marked the area when Spitfire was underground, as if reluctant to give up her new-found role. However, it was clear that Spitfire would remain the dominant female in the pack and when she appeared more frequently above ground, Soda gave up her marking behaviour.

A week later Gretel, the most subordinate of the females, also had a litter. I now wondered whether Havoc's role would be re-enacted by Spitfire. However, the opposite happened. Not only did Gretel take advantage of Spitfire's absence hunting with the males to steal the dominant female's pups, but unlike Havoc, she did not kill them but adopted all ten. Whether Spitfire realized what had happened I do not know, but in any case she was unable to investigate since the subordinate female vigorously blocked the way into the narrow passage of the den. Thus Spitfire was left without pups, whilst Gretel had twenty. By now Spitfire's puppies were four and Gretel's three weeks old and a few days later they emerged into daylight for the first time.

I had been worried that it might be impossible for me to tell which pups belonged to which mother. However, this proved to be easy, for not only was there a slight difference in size, but also a striking variation in colouring. Spitfire's pups had large patches of white, like their mother, while Gretel's offspring were uniformly dark. But though this was clear to me, I do not think it was at all so to the mothers, for from then on they competed for each and every pup. This would not have been too bad if they had merely tried to outdo each other in suckling, but they also frequently engaged in tugs-of-war, with one holding on to a pup's rump, tail or hind-leg while the other gripped its head and pulled in the opposite direction. Luckily the older female, Gretel, seemed to sense when the pup was about to be ripped apart and would concede victory.

The problem was that each female wanted all twenty pups in her own den and so each spent her time stealing pups from the vicinity of the other's burrow and carrying them to her own. Not infrequently they passed each other midway. Seeing the two females compete in this way, their respective mates joined in. However, it soon appeared that the whole situation was too complicated for them. They quickly forgot to which den they were supposed to be carrying the pups, so Gretel's mate might carry a pup to Spitfire's den, while Spitfire's mate was just as likely to do the opposite. Sometimes, in fact, they took them from a den only to deposit them halfway and so confuse the situation even more. Then gradually, as the days went by, both females tired of their efforts and shared the pups on a reasonably friendly basis.

Puppies are rarely left alone at a den. Usually when the pack goes off to hunt, their mother stays with them. However, it is sometimes obvious that a mother would like to join the hunt and then, if any other dog shows any indication of being ready to stay behind, it may be left in charge. Occasionally, especially in small packs, the pups may be left completely on their own.

The main potential danger to the pups is the hyena. It is not unusual to see one or more hyenas approach a dog den; however, even a single dog has little trouble in driving it off, for the dog moves much faster and can dash in and bite it from behind. I have seen a wild dog tear open a hyena's bottom in this way.

The relationship between hyenas and wild dogs is complex and varied. I suspect many pups fall victim to hyenas when they are between four and twelve months old and no longer live in a den. At night, especially, it is common to find hyenas following a pack of wild dogs and trying to take over their kills. In addition wild dog dung is a delicacy to hyenas; so much so that they often creep up to sleeping dogs and lick their bottoms.

In these cases the hyena is parasitic towards the wild dog, but I remember once seeing a somewhat upside-down relationship. A wild dog had lost its pack. For many hours it searched in vain, uttering calls of distress. Soon two hyenas appeared on the scene and, approaching the lone dog, tried repeatedly to lick its bottom. Invariably the dog responded by attacking them and finally, after an hour or so, the two hyenas gave up and started to walk away. At this point, however, rather than be left alone, the dog followed them. When the hyenas reached a pool of water and lay down in it to rest, the dog joined them. Having been attacked before, the hyenas reacted nervously to the dog's behaviour and left the pool to search for another place to rest. The dog immediately followed them. For the next hour the hyenas acted nervously, but finally they calmed down and the two species slept side by side for the rest of the day.

Much nonsense is talked about the hunting behaviour of wild dogs. It is said, for instance, that once a prey has been selected it has no chance of escape, for the dogs will relentlessly pursue it in relays, some dogs running slowly at the back and then taking over when the front ones tire. Another belief is that potential prey animals panic at the mere sight of wild dogs. In fact about half the animals pursued manage to outrun the dogs and thus escape. Nor do they panic on seeing the dogs. Flight distances vary, but Thomson Gazelles may let dogs get within one hundred yards before fleeing, while zebras sometimes allow them to within thirty yards. The origin of the myth that dogs hunt in relays is easy to understand. When a pack of dogs pursues a Thomson Gazelle, their most common prey, the gazelle often runs in large zig-zags or describes a circle. By cutting corners, dogs running at the back may end up in front of the pack. Usually, however, this merely spurs the original front-runners to put on extra speed and so to end up in front again.

I have frequently timed wild dogs and found they ran almost consistently at 30 m.p.h. with occasional spurts of over 35 m.p.h. I have timed Thomson Gazelles at 45 m.p.h. but this was over short distances. The longest chase I have actually measured was $3\frac{1}{2}$ miles in which a Grant's Gazelle, which the Genghis pack was chasing, in the end managed to escape. I roughly calculated another chase to be five miles, but this sort of guess is dangerous for it is easy to over-estimate. The same is true of the time it takes wild dogs to kill their prey. It has been commonly said that this often takes fifteen minutes. In fact it is unusual for kills to take longer than $2\frac{1}{2}$ to $3\frac{1}{2}$ minutes, during which time the prey is so shocked that it is doubtful whether it feels any pain.

An interesting aspect of wild dog behaviour is that, once the puppies are old enough to keep up with a hunt or are taken to a kill by the adults, they have priority in feeding. While they feed, the adults stand back; in fact if any adult tries to join them, it is attacked by the youngsters as a group and sometimes by some of the adults too. If the prey is small, the adults will hunt again for their own needs.

This can cause confusion. I remember one year when there were many orphaned wildebeest calves wandering through the bush country around Ndutu. The pack of dogs I was watching consisted of ten adults and ten half-grown pups. During one hunt they chased a wildebeest calf right through my camp, jumping over the guyropes of my tents as they did so. After they had caught the calf, the pups took over and started to eat. Almost immediately the adults saw another calf and started their next hunt. Seeing their elders rush off, the pups left their meal and hurried after them. Of course, having hardly eaten yet, the pups took over the second kill as well. Again the adults spotted another calf; again the pups followed and for a third time took over the kill. This time, however, they managed to stuff themselves before the adults hunted for a fourth time, and so finally the latter managed to eat themselves.

Wasteful though this was, I was not sorry that the dogs had killed these four calves. The only other possibilities for the orphan wildebeests were to be killed by another predator or to starve.

During my work on wild dogs I occasionally saw packs meet each other. Invariably the larger pack chased away the smaller. The most extraordinary meeting I witnessed occurred when the Genghis pack found the den of the Pimpernel pack. This was at the time the two females, Gretel and Spitfire, had their pups.

It was four o'clock in the afternoon. The pups had not been above ground for some time, but the six adults were in the open and stood close together sniffing at a tuft of grass. They did not notice that, three hundred yards from them, nine dogs of the Genghis pack were stealthily creeping forward through the high grass. The invaders remained so close together that their bodies almost touched; every movement they made was in slow motion and seemed filled with menace.

Suddenly the Pimpernel pack looked in their direction. Without hesitation the Genghis pack charged and the Pimpernel pack fled. The main body of the Genghis pack concentrated on the mother, Spitfire, who ran away with two of the males from her pack, the third fleeing in a different direction. The remaining two females of the Pimpernel pack, Gretel and Soda, rushed down into the dens in which the pack's puppies were sleeping. They were chased by two of the Genghis pack, but the pursuers seemed confused when the two females disappeared, as if not realizing that they had gone underground. After a brief hesitation they joined the rest of their pack in pursuit of Spitfire and the two males.

After the dogs had run five hundred yards, Spitfire and her two males reached the tree line around Ndutu and disappeared from sight. At this the Genghis pack stopped. Then they suddenly noticed the third male of the Pimpernel pack, who had run in the opposite direction and now stood alone in the open, looking back at them. Immediately the Genghis pack turned and ran towards him. The lone male broke into flight. This chase lasted for several miles and caused panic amongst the herds of gazelles which fled in all directions away from the running dogs. A Golden Jackal, too, was taken by surprise and raced flat out for two hundred yards before literally diving into its den, sending a large squirt of dust flying out backwards.

At last the Genghis pack came across a puddle of water and briefly stopped to drink. When they looked up they saw the lone black shape, still peering at them from two hundred yards further on. At once they continued the pursuit. By now, however, they had lost the lone dog, for when the black shape fled, it stuck its thin tail straight into the air. The Genghis pack, realizing their prey had somehow been metamorphosed into a warthog, called off the hunt.

Soon afterwards they headed back in the direction of the Pimpernel pack dens.

I wondered if they knew of their existence. Apparently not, for when they came within a hundred yards of the dens they lay down to rest. Sleeping in the high grass they were now invisible, except from very close by.

An hour later, Spitfire appeared from among the trees and cautiously moved to the plain towards her den. Every few steps she stopped, wagged her tail, and looked all around her. Finally she began to walk forward quite briskly, but then stopped, looked around, and nervously went back a few steps. Suddenly Soda appeared at the entrance to her den, followed by some pups. Spitfire, as if reassured, joined her with fast springy steps. As she reached the den, Gretel also emerged and the three females stood together, looking around nervously. From where they stood they could not see the Genghis pack, still asleep only one hundred yards away.

When the Genghis pack woke up and greeted each other, the three females of the Pimpernel pack were underground. At first it seemed as if the Genghis pack would not find their dens, for they moved past them and went on about two hundred yards. Suddenly they stopped and sniffed the ground; then turned and headed straight towards the dens. They were now down wind of these and it looked as if they were guided to them by the smell. Again the pack moved forward in a tight group, their movements slow and threatening. Nothing could stop them finding the three females and the pups, trapped underground. Sixty yards from the den, the front dogs sank down on to their tummies, silent and still. Then they slowly rose again and stalked forward. Havoc, the dominant female, looked less at ease than the others and I noticed at one stage that her posture was strange, for she leant backwards whilst moving forwards, as if demonstrating the conflicts within her; the urge, perhaps, to avoid a possibly dangerous confrontation battling with the urge to go forward and investigate.

When the Genghis pack reached the dens, they continued to move in slow motion, warily sniffing the ground around them. Soon two of the males found one of the dens, and, pausing briefly, went down together. There was complete silence. It seemed the two males did not go far, for they both soon emerged, still silent and moving slowly. Then Havoc found another den and stared down it. Suddenly a short alarm bark broke the stillness. The adult dogs of the Genghis pack ran off a short distance, while the pups fled pell mell for a few hundred yards.

The adults came to a jerky halt and stared back at the den from which the alarm bark had come. Then they went back to the dens, moving more quickly now. On reaching them, various dogs went a little way down, being met by vicious growls from the trapped females. I felt sure that the Genghis pack would now attack the Pimpernel females and their pups, but in fact nothing of the sort happened. They spent some time looking down the dens and then trotted off as if nothing had happened. Finally they disappeared from sight across the plains.

It was not until another twelve hours had passed that the three Pimpernel pack males returned to the dens, emerging nervously and ghostlike from the early morning mist. The females reacted in fright at their appearance, but once they realized who it was, they greeted each other with frenzied, birdlike twitters and much licking. Once again the pack was united.

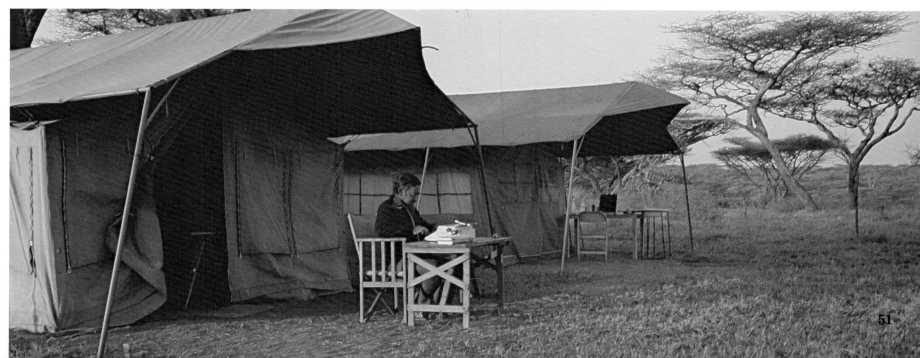

Lions

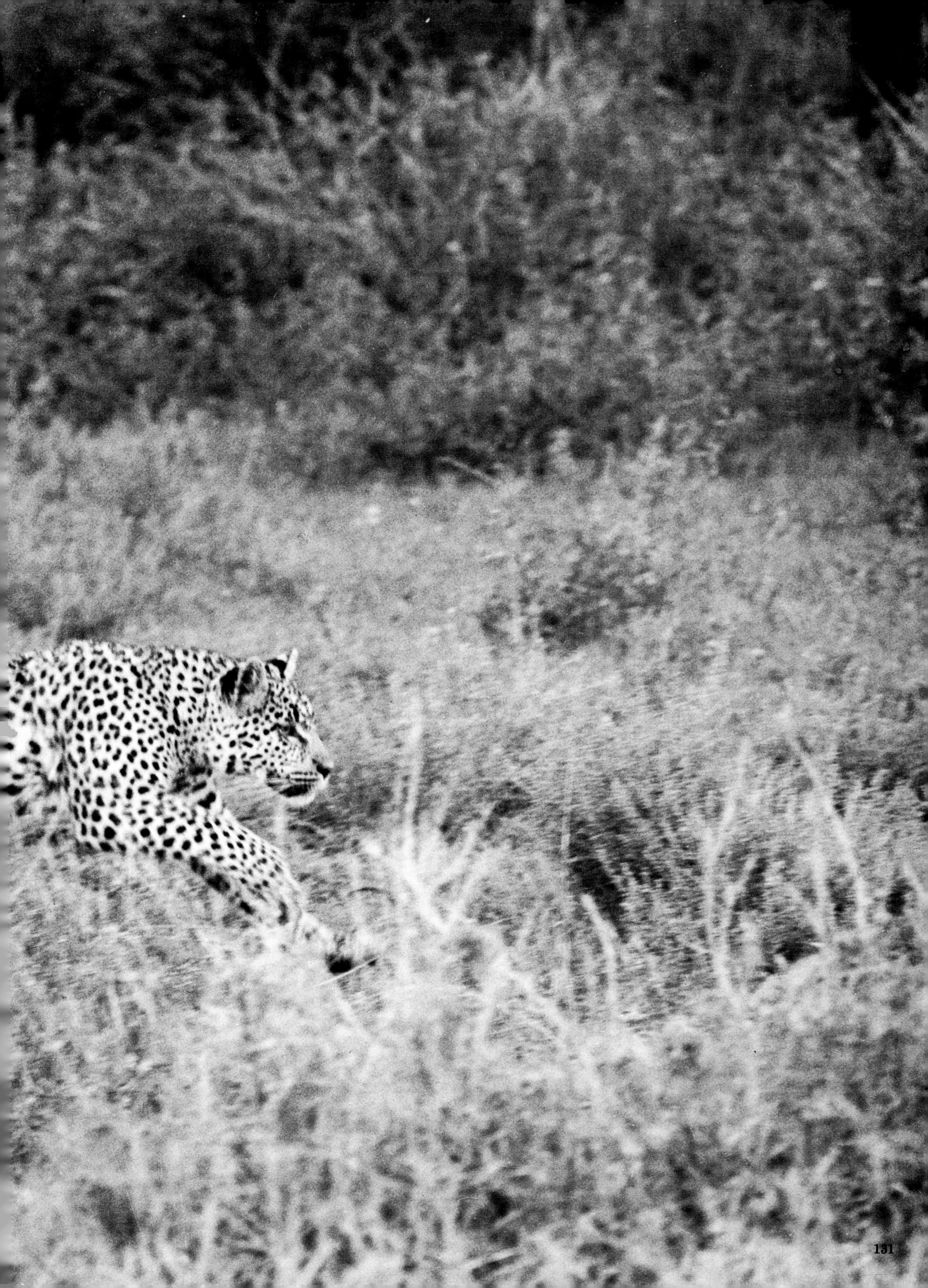

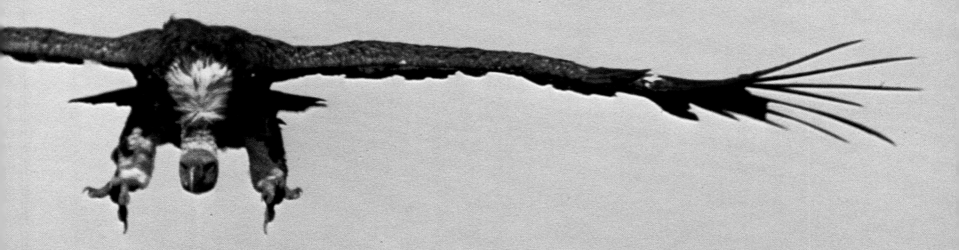

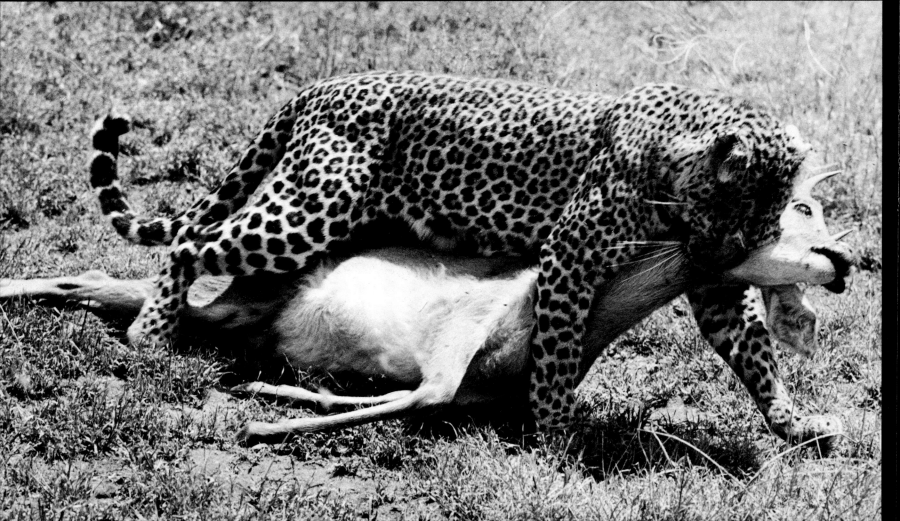

139

Cheetahs

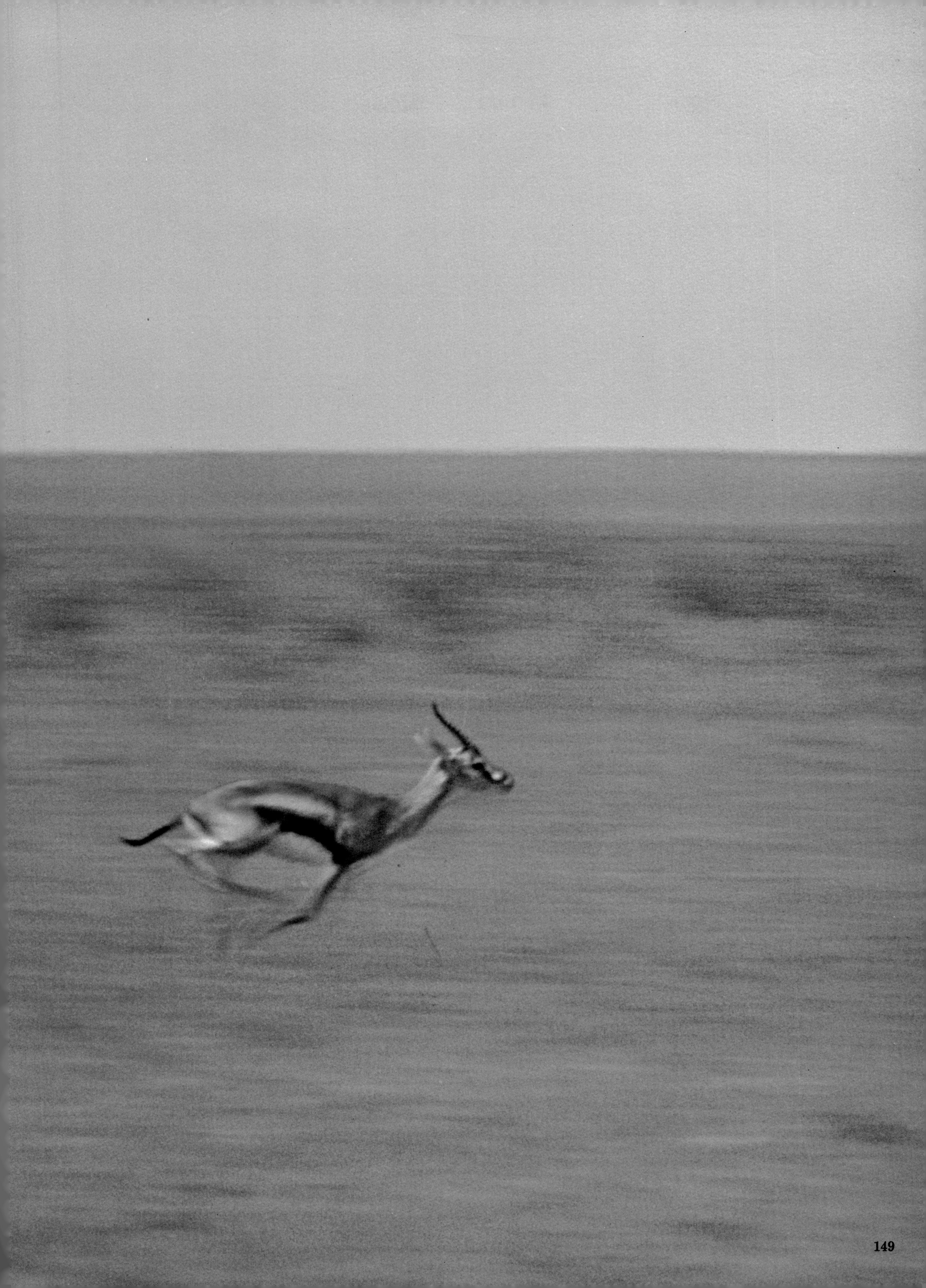

Jackals

List of plates

Bold figures refer to page numbers

48-9 During a search for predators, which sometimes might cover a hundred miles in a day, I pause to look over a vast expanse of the shortgrass plains, South West of the Gol Mountains, which are visible in the background.

> Photo: Robert Caputo.
> Copyright: Hugo van Lawick

50-1a Formations of rocks called kopjes, some large, some small, are scattered throughout the Serengeti. They give a good view over the surrounding countryside, but one needs to be cautious for they are also a favourite habitat of lions, leopards and snakes such as cobras.

> Photo: Robert Caputo.
> Copyright: Hugo van Lawick

51b Much of my photography is done from a car. Most animals get so used to my vehicle that they ignore it completely.

> Photo: Robert Caputo.
> Copyright: Hugo van Lawick

51c Giraffes regularly visit my camp as do lions, hyenas and jackals; the last three species usually at night.

51d Situated in the shade of acacia trees overlooking Lake Ndutu, my camp was an ideal place for writing this book.

> Photo: Robert Caputo.
> Copyright: Hugo van Lawick

Lions

52-3 (*2 plates*) The number of adult males in a pride can vary from one to six or occasionally even more. I suspect they are usually brothers or at least related. Young males leave the pride, probably driven out, when two or three years old, and become nomads until they are old enough to try to take over another pride from its resident males.

54–5 Two male lions with a problem: four lionesses in their pride had come into heat at the same time. The dominant male on the left laid claim to three females, while the subordinate male took possession of the remaining one. (pp.15–16)

56–7 The dominant male was however frustrated; the female he wanted to mate with was not interested and went to sleep – or at least pretended to.

58–9 The other females in turn tried to persuade the dominant male to mate with them, but, snarling threateningly, he indicated that he was not interested – even though the female he wanted, continued to ignore him.

60–1 (*four plates*) Whilst approaching his favoured female, the frustrated dominant male forcefully rebuffed one of the other lionesses, which crouched submissively at first but then hit back at him.

62–3 Over the next four days and nights the dominant male persisted in his vain pursuit of the lioness he fancied – while ignoring the other females which continually tried to allure him.

64–5 The subordinate male was able to mate, but he had a problem too; his female kept trying to slip past him and join the dominant male with the other three females.

66–7 The subordinate male got little sleep because of the need to keep constant watch over his female.

68-9 Finally the subordinate male closed his eyes for too long while his female pretended to sleep.

70-1 (*four plates*) When his female joined the others the subordinate male rushed after her, but the dominant male fought him and forced him to retreat.

72-3 Having lost his female and his fight with the dominant male, the subordinate male exhibited his frustration by rubbing his hind feet on the ground.

74-5 The dominant male now had four females. Three were keen to be mated, but he was still only interested in the fourth, which continued to reject him.

76-7 Of all the cats, lions are the most sociable in their behaviour. Mothers in a pride form nursery groups and cubs may suckle from any of the lactating females.

78-9 Many lion cubs on the Serengeti spend the first month or so of their lives living amongst rocks which contain small caves and crevices, ideal hiding places for them while their mother is hunting.

80-1 Near my camp at Ndutu the lionesses often used a marsh as a place in which to give birth and to hide their young cubs.

82-3 Young cubs are inquisitive but cautious when they first view man but, providing they are not molested, they soon get used to my car and normally ignore me.

84 Lion cubs spend much time clambering up the trunks of small trees.

85 Lake Ndutu, where the four lionesses and their sixteen cubs lived just below my camp. (p. 17)

86 (*two plates*) Lions will not normally tolerate vultures close to their kill.

87 To avoid the heat, lions often rest in the shade of acacia trees and will drag a kill to a tree if possible.

88-9 (*two plates*) On the right a colourful male Agama Lizard. I have seen these lizards crawl over resting lions in order to catch the flies which have settled on their hides. The lions normally ignore them, but in one case I saw a lizard snap too hard, pinching the lioness as it did so and provoking a threatening snarl. (pp. 19–20)

90-1 Like all cats, lions spend much time sleeping, but they are unusual in that they often lie close together.

92 (*two plates*)   A young lion chooses a difficult way to get past one of its siblings.

93   The adult lions of the Ndutu pride sometimes rest in trees. Their cubs usually try to follow their example.

94-5   A lion will prey on giraffes, but risks receiving a kick powerful enough to smash in its face or break a leg.

96-7   The Thomson Gazelle is a common prey of lions, especially near water holes. The wood ibis in the foreground ignores the hunt.

98-9   Lions and hyenas often compete over each other's kills, and not uncommonly lionesses must make way for hyenas, especially if the latter appear on the scene in large numbers.

100-1   A male with his pride of females.

102-3 (*three plates*)   A male lion sniffs at a female's bottom, apparently trying to ascertain whether she is coming into heat. He then pulls a 'Flemen face', an expression used by many animals in connection with sex.

104-5 During the wildebeest migration, great herds of wildebeests cross Lake Ndutu. Often many drown and calves and mothers get separated. The orphan calves provide easy prey for the predators living around the lake.

106-7 (*three plates*) Wildebeest play. Many people consider them to be the clowns of the animal world. Certainly it is not uncommon to see them frolic like this.

(Copyright: National Geographic Society.)

106-7 Whilst lions are courting, which may last as long as ten days, they do not hunt.

108-9 Having seen vultures landing, a lion runs across the plain to take over the carcass found by the birds.

110-11 Like all the other carnivores, with the possible exception of the cheetah, lions will scavenge, eating animals killed by others or which have died naturally.

112-13 During the dry season flamingoes feed in the small pools in the marshes around Ndutu. With normal prey scarce, the lions hunt these birds.

114-15 Most of the lions' activity takes place after the sun has set.

Leopards

116-17 Leopards are solitary by nature. This female was searching for a hare which had hidden in the high grass and managed to escape.

118-19 A female leopard and her practically full grown son. I was able to find them almost daily for a period of six months, something I had been told would be impossible before I started the study. (p. 22)

120-21 (*two plates*) The leopard son playing with its mother. Like a human's finger prints, each leopard has its own pattern of spots.

122-23 There was a close bond between the mother and her cub, shown in their play and in the way they frequently licked each other.

124 The superb camouflage of a leopard is shown in this picture, where a female is lying over the broken branch half way up the tree on the right. Her cub in the vegetation above is almost invisible.

125 Leopards spend a great deal of their time sleeping, both in trees and on the ground.

126-27 Certain trees within her territory were preferred by the mother leopard and, once I knew which ones, it was easier to find her. The search was somewhat simplified by driving against the light when the leopard's silhouette would show up more clearly.

128-29 Trees make a good vantage point from which to spot prey. Leopards will often travel only short distances at a time, climbing trees every fifty yards or so, and looking around for potential prey.

130-31 In hunting adult prey the leopard first creeps as close as possible, then runs towards it at surprising speed, which, however, it can only keep up for a short distance.

132-33 The Serval, about twice the size of a domestic cat, uses its large, sensitive ears to locate its prey. Yet a leopard can move so silently, that Servals are sometimes caught by them.

133 The Caracal, with pointed ears like those of a Lynx, is usually a shy creature, seldom seen. This one was lying motionless, waiting for rodents to appear from their holes.

134-35 The mother leopard with her prey, an African Wild Cat, which in appearance is similar to a domestic tabby. Leopards kill most of their prey by biting into the victims' throats.

136-37 (*two plates*) On the left a White Headed Vulture takes to the air. It is said occasionally to catch its own prey, but I have never observed this nor met anyone who has. On the right a Ruppel's Griffon Vulture ready to land.

138 The mother leopard with a reedbuck which she is dragging to a tree. Unless she can get it to safety she is liable to lose her kill to hyenas.

139 The mother leopard pauses to drink.

140-41 Vultures usually start to settle for the night before the sun sets.

Cheetahs

142-43 A female cheetah yawning before setting off to hunt. Females usually lead a solitary life except when they have cubs.

144-45 Thomson Gazelles are the most common prey of cheetahs on the Serengeti. In the rainy season over three quarters of a million of these gazelles may graze on the shortgrass plains.

146-47 A mother cheetah stares as she spots potential prey. Her cubs, sitting behind her, will wait while the mother hunts.

148-49 I have timed Thomson Gazelles at 45 m.p.h. Cheetahs have been timed at 70 m.p.h., but can only keep up this speed for a short distance.

150-51 A lone cheetah stalks its prey, remaining motionless when the prey looks in its direction. Most prey find it hard to distinguish carnivores which do not move – even if they are very close to them.

152-53 A cheetah chases a Thomson Gazelle calf. Mother cheetahs will take such calves alive to their cubs, giving the young cheetahs an opportunity to exercise their hunting skills.

154 Cheetahs usually kill their prey by biting into the throat as lions and leopards do.

155 A Rupell's Griffon Vulture preening itself in mid-air.

156-57 Three sub-adult cheetahs peacefully share a kill.

158-59 Cheetahs will chase vultures from the vicinity of their kills but, unlike the other African predators, have never been observed to scavenge themselves.

160-61 When I first suggested, in 1962, that cheetahs would take large prey, no one I spoke to believed it. Here a cheetah chases into a large herd of adult wildebeests. They have recently been seen to pull down full grown hartebeests and zebras.

162-63 Cheetah cubs will often involve their mother in their games.

164-65 Young cheetahs, even when sub-adult, spend much time in play. Most play, however, involves chases, undoubtedly good practice for serious hunting.

166-67 (*three plates*) I thought I had found a male attempting to mate a female, something rarely observed before, but I then discovered the cheetahs involved were merely male siblings exhibiting homosexual behaviour. (p. 30)

168-69 (*four plates*) One of the two brother cheetahs at Ndutu attacks the four sub-adult males. The next day, the four youngsters left the area with their mother, which had been attacked by the other brother. (p. 30)

170-71 A cheetah family resting on a termite mound – often favoured by cheetahs since they afford a good view over the surrounding countryside.

Hyenas

172-73 Hyenas are numerous on the floor of the Ngorongoro Crater, living in clans up to one hundred strong. Neighbouring clans are aggressive towards each other, and not uncommonly engage in 'warfare'. Probably as a result, hyena dens tend to be situated in the centre of a clan's territory.

174-75 The Ngorongoro Crater. Once a gigantic volcano, the top crumbled and formed the crater floor, one hundred square miles in size.

176-77 Black at birth, a hyena cub's spots start to appear when it is about two months old. Possibly due to the aggressive nature of adult hyenas at a kill, cubs depend on their mother's milk until they are about eighteen months old and half her size.

178-79 Members of a hyena clan, in this case the Lake Side Clan, regularly patrol the borders of their territory.

180-81 Once believed to be cowardly scavengers, hyenas in fact are efficient hunters and far from cowardly. I have seen them attack rhino calves on a number of occasions, in spite of the proximity of the mother.

182-83 A group of zebras graze tranquilly on the Serengeti plains.

184-85 While a lone hyena may tackle a wildebeest, when pursuing zebras they usually hunt in groups. Hyenas may set out specifically to hunt zebras, ignoring other species. It is not uncommon to see other animals, such as wildebeests in this instance, ignore a hunt in which they are not the chosen prey.

186-87 Hyenas kill most of their prey by eating into the groin and stomach. Whilst unpleasant to watch, it is doubtful if the prey feels much pain.

188-89 A lone hyena can have difficulties when competing over a kill with vultures and may retreat from their sharp beaks.

190 A Marabou Stork tries to steal a scrap of meat from a vulture. Marabou Storks are unable to tear meat from a carcass and so depend on snatching scraps which they swallow whole.

191 About ten years ago, Jane Goodall and I discovered that Egyptian Vultures throw stones to crack open ostrich eggs, making them one of the few animals known to use an object as a tool.

(Copyright: National Geographic Society)

192-93 (*two plates*)   Male hyenas and sub-adult females hunt flamingoes in the Ngorongoro Crater Lake.

194-95   After heavy rain on the Serengeti, two hyenas enjoy the water.

196   A member of the Scratching Rocks Clan crosses the Munge River, which flows through the clan's territory in the Ngorongoro Crater.

197   Thomson Gazelles are a common prey of hyenas, especially on the Serengeti.

198-99   Members of the Scratching Rocks Clan regularly drink from the Munge River at about sunset, before they start their night activities.

200-201 (*above*)   While not hesitating to tackle a fleeing bull wildebeest, hyenas are more cautious about attacking one which stands still and faces them.

200-201 (*below*) Having successfully pulled down a wildebeest just over their border, members of the Scratching Rocks Clan are approached by their neighbours, the Lake Side Clan, and ultimately have to make way for them.

Jackals

203 A Golden Jackal cub.

204-5 The open plains near Ndutu. Two species of jackals are common near my camp: the Silver Back, which mainly inhabit the tree and bush country, and the Golden, which live mainly on the open plains.

206-7 Like wild dogs, jackals usually suckle their cubs in a standing position. Like wild dogs, too, the youngsters start eating meat at three to four weeks old and stop suckling when still under three months.

208-9 The young mother jackal I was watching was not very experienced in carrying cubs to a new den. Jackals regularly move their offspring from one den to another; I suspect to reduce the risk of other predators, especially hyenas, finding them.

210-11 Adult jackals will attack and chase off hyenas which approach their den. They are able to do this because they move faster than a hyena and can nip with their sharp teeth at the larger predator's bottom and ankles.

212-13 The female and male Golden Jackal which I was watching on the Serengeti.

214   Ostrich feathers are favourite toys for jackal cubs and wild dogs.

215 (*above*)   Jackal cubs howling.

215 (*below*)   Jackals in the Ngorongoro Crater often hunt snakes, which they kill by shaking them briefly but vigorously and then letting go before they can retaliate. This they repeat a number of times. On this occasion, the jackal had let go, but the snake briefly got caught around its neck, before it slipped off and tried unsuccessfully to escape.

216–17 (*three plates*)   Normally, Golden Jackals ignore hares, which are too fast for them to catch easily.

218–19   A group of jackals begin a game on the Serengeti plains.

220–21   Golden Jackals snapping at bothersome flies.

222–23   A female Grants Gazelle, accompanied by a male, approaches a Golden Jackal which is getting close to her fawn, hidden in the grass.

224–25 (*three plates*)   Golden Jackals often hunt Thomson Gazelle fawns. While one jackal of a pair is pursued by the mother gazelle, the other catches the fawn.

(Second plate by Diana Saltoon
Copyright: Hugo van Lawick)

226–27 Vultures and jackals commonly compete at a kill, sometimes jackals must make way if the vultures are on the scene in large numbers.

229 Eagles seem to be the most common predators of jackal cubs.

230–31 It is not unusual to see Silver Back Jackals in large numbers around a kill. Due to their speed jackals are often able to share in a lion's kill, darting in to grab a morsel and then rushing off with it.

Wild dogs

232–33 Two dogs of the Pimpernel pack greet each other after resting near the dens.

234–35 In the Pimpernel pack both lactating females wanted all twenty pups in their own den and so each spent much time stealing pups from the vicinity of the other's burrow. (p. 44)

236 Pups rush to their mother as she is about to regurgitate food for them.

237 (*above*) Both pups and adults will often tear meat in 'tugs of war'. Wild dogs rarely fight each other over food, which sets them apart from most other species of animal.

237 (*below*)   As the pups grow older, they spend less time in their den, often resting in the open. Unless it is hot, wild dogs tend to rest in small piles together; each age group, however, normally forms a separate group.

238–39   Part of the largest litter I have seen. The mother had given birth to sixteen pups.

240–41   During the rains, the wildebeest migration, over one million strong, congregates on the short grass plains near my camp.

242–43   While the front two dogs attempt to grab a yearling wildebeest's ears, in order to pull it over on its side, others in the pack move in at the rear.

245   When wild dogs make a large kill, such as a wildebeest, they are not able to eat everything themselves and so much is left to the vultures.

246–47 (*two plates*)   The speciality of the Genghis pack was hunting zebras. Like the twitch used by man on horses, a wild dog holds a zebra immobile by clinging on to its upper lip.

248–49   In a last desperate attempt to escape, a Thomson Gazelle jumps over a wild dog, performing a complete roll as it does so. Going at full speed – about 35 mph – the dog was unable to turn immediately and ran on for a few yards before rushing back and catching the gazelle.

250-51 The end of possibly the longest hunt I have seen – about five miles. The prey, an adult male Grants Gazelle, was finally caught when it stumbled in a hole and broke one of its legs.

252-53 The Genghis pack became so accustomed to me that I could follow them day and night.